The Grown-up Girl's Guide to Life

JACQUI RIPLEY

PIATKUS

First published in 2007 by
Piatkus Books Ltd
5 Windmill Street
London W1T 2JA
Email: info@piatkus.co.uk

The moral right of the author has been asserted
A catalogue record for this book is available from
the British Library.

ISBN13: 978 0 7499 2779 0

Edited by Jan Cutler
Text design by Goldust Design

This book has been printed on paper manufactured with
respect for the environment using wood from managed
sustainable resources.

Printed and bound in Great Britain by
William Clowes Ltd, Beccles, Suffolk

Contents

Acknowledgements

Thank you to my editor Alice Davis, my husband John for many things, but namely for advising me how to handle builders for inclusion in this book, and my lovely son Dylan for constantly reminding me how funny life can be.

Introduction

When I was initially mulling over an idea for my next book with Alice, my editor, I said that there was a new hybrid of females who slotted into a social demographic that were too old to be thought of as girls but too young to be classed as fully signed-up adult women. 'They're grown-up girls,' I said. Even if you're officially labelled a woman, isn't there a part of you that still feels girlie and not yet ready to trade your champagne-like giggles for polite laughing or your cute cocktails for a fine wine? So these are the people who I've aimed this book at – girls like you who still want plenty of fun in their life but with a sprinkling of grown-up responsibility, too.

And now for the subject matter: life – a little word but a very big subject to tackle. When Alice and I were bouncing ideas off each other I definitely said that I wanted to write a Grown-up Girl's Guide to something, but I didn't yet know what. 'Life,' she said, 'Every grown-up girl wants to know what to do in life.' First off, I won't be afraid to admit the idea scared me. After all, what did I know about dishing up advice about life? I'm not a psychologist or somebody with lots of letters after my name. But then I thought, 'Well, I know a lot about grown-up girls,' as I've worked on and for various magazines where I've been privy to the insights of what grown-up girls want and need from life, what they worry about, what they want to know and, more importantly, want they want to read about. In the course of my work I've also had, and still continue to have, many interesting conversations with fashion designers and make-up artists as well as nutritionists, psychologists, sexual psychotherapists, dermatologists and other eminent ologists! And, after thinking about it, I jotted down some subjects I thought I would like to cover. I ended up with four pages of them! Of course, I couldn't write on every single subject, so I cherry-picked the ones I thought would be relevant and useful – from the serious to the not so serious. After all, who doesn't want to know the golden rules of buying a bikini, fabulous looking hair, finding a job you will love, to getting promoted or cleaning your house in just an hour?

Ultimately, life is there to be lived fully and it's never one smooth ride – if only! Chances are it can wind up a bumpy trip with surprising twists, turns and serious detours. And, let's face it, no one hands out a map to living your life, you just have to get by and find your own way. Which is where my book comes in. I have addressed all the little dilemmas sent to try and test us and offer little pearls of wisdom that I've picked up from my many years of listening, jotting down advice from experts and writing on grown-up girls' issues. Although it might not turn your life around it can at least help to put a positive (and sometimes very funny) spin on how you see and handle things.

I've enjoyed writing this book, so I hope you enjoy reading it, too. But what I really hope is that out of all the subjects I've chosen to write about there will be some pieces of advice, general patterns of thought and wry observations that will help make your own life better, more pleasurable, more intuitive, more successful and, above all, that little bit more grown up.

CHAPTER 1
Body, Beauty and Boobs

A life lesson in looking (and feeling) good naked

Somewhere from the time of Eve, who walked around the Garden of Eden with nothing but leaves to hide her modesty, our perception of what makes a beautiful body has gone seriously screwy. To get naked and be happy with our God-given lot, we have ultimately come to believe that we need to measure up to a super skinny who seemingly shops in the kids' section for her jeans. The upshot? We process the images of (airbrushed) perfection way too literally in our minds to the point where it becomes harder to accept the bodies we are actually blessed with. But feeling sexy while being naked isn't so hard. In fact, it's dead easy. For a nude awakening, start to shed your hang-ups with these stripped-down confidence boosters.

Body-worship yourself

Undress and look at yourself in the mirror. What do you see? Chances are you've zoned straight in on your wobbly tummy and cellulite. Am I right? If so, quit dissecting yourself like you're a biology experiment. Focusing on bits of your body you're not so keen on prevents you from moving forward and embracing the bits about yourself you think are OK. Get a real-woman reality check, too. Next time you're shuffling into a pair of jeans in a communal changing room, sweep your eyes around the room and appreciate the beauty in every shape and size. Next, look to using some props – a bit like a burlesque dancer! If you're one of those girls who always flicks the switch off before you get naked in front of your man, then dressing up while you're getting naked can work wonders. Wearing sparkling earrings, for example, throws light back into your face and makes your eyes twinkle. And getting high on heels and walking around in them with little else makes legs look long and lithe. As the old adage goes: if you feel fabulous, you'll look fabulous.

Think yourself sexy

Play your body to the crowd and reap the adulation! Shuffling around with stooped shoulders and a baggy old jumper does nothing for your body image, let alone putting you in touch with your inner flirt. Full-on flirting can be your fast track to feeling great clothed, which in turn makes you feel great naked. The very act of flirting allows you to fall in love with yourself for who you are – not who you think you should be. Supercharge your body language and a good sense of body image will naturally start to follow. Become more confident with your body by choosing clothes that celebrate your curves – a scoop-necked top instead of a polo neck, for example. Next, throw your shoulders back, lift your head high and smile

– at everyone. This sense of playfulness doubles up as sexy role play and does wonders for your esteem.

Feel (very) comfortable in your skin

Make your own definition of beauty. You are responsible for making yourself feel good – so take control and don't let a dress size dictate how happy you are with your shape. Build body confidence by acting like a nudist in your own house. It's totally liberating. Vacuum naked, talk on the phone naked, do a spot of yoga naked. But, best of all, shake your booty naked. Dancing without clothes makes you feel unbelievably happy and confident.

Be naughty, but feel nice

Bypass sexy underwear and wear nothing under your clothing. Leave your knickers at home and meet your date or even have a meeting with your boss with a bare butt! Even if they don't know – and why should they unless you do a

Sharon Stone number – it gives you a (mini) thrill as well as being your first step to relaxing about your body.

LIFE-LONG TIP

Be your own stagehand. When actresses get naked, studios hire the best lighting technicians and make-up artists. Why should it be any different for you? Soft lighting equals soft shadows, which flatters naked skin.

Next time you're 'entertaining', dim the lights. Shimmy up your skin, too, by slathering on an illuminating lotion.

A life lesson in a surgery-free boob job

Small breasts vs big breasts: who cares what size you've been handed out as long as they're healthy, perky(ish) and look great saddled up in a bra? Every girl likes her breasts to look their best, and with so many clothes now placing their emphasis firmly on the boobs, it pays to know how to show them off in the best possible (lime)light. Here's how to enhance the pair Mother Nature (not a surgeon) gave you.

A show of support

Rule number one: you want your girlie assets to jiggle, not dangle. One of the reasons breasts become droopy is down to the bra – or lack of it. Unless you've got fried eggs, all breasts need uplift, and going braless may make you feel like a free-spirited-bra-burning babe but in reality it does nothing for your look. Seeking out a properly fitting bra is not purely cosmetic, it will also play dividends in retaining breast firmness over time. Most department stores run a free bra-fitting service for customers, so make use of it. Invest in a sports bra, too, as excessive breast movement can irreversibly stretch the Cooper ligaments. This means that once the ligaments are stretched, the breasts will sag and nothing can lift them up again apart from surgery. A good-fitting style will provide support and comfort, so you can forget you're wearing it and focus on your sport. Look for an encapsulation-style sports bra that separates and supports to avoid the 'uni-boob' look and gives an excellent uplift for medium and high-impact activities.

Get all touchy feely

A beautiful bosom is a caressed bosom! Well, that's the French thinking, anyway. Massaging the bust professionally with uplifting creams is de rigueur in France and seen as something natural and so much simpler than anything involving scalpels and implants. Generally it seems we are traditionally shy in booking ourselves in for such intimate bare-it-all treatments, but, rest assured, the perkier-bust massage trick can be carried out away from the therapist's eyes and in the safety of your own bathroom. Simply buy a bust-firming gel or serum, warm it in the palm of your hands and then start applying it to your breasts, massaging the area your bra would cover. Take time over your décolletage, too (that's the area that is shown when you wear a low-necked top) – it can look crêpey as it's prone to sun damage and general neglect, reducing the elasticity and therefore the tightness in the skin. When massaging from the underside of your boobs, sweep up towards your décolletage and then fan out the motion towards the lymph nodes under your armpits to rid them of toxins.

Fall into doing this ritual every morning or night after a bath or shower. It can also be one of your breast defences against checking any irregularities such as unusual lumps or thickening.

Fake it till you make it

OK, I'm not talking something as crass as stuffing tissues into your bra, but a little make-up wizardry can do wonders to create an illusion of a bigger cup size. To fake a 'curvy' cleavage, dip a big soft, fluffy brush into a light-coloured bronzer and dust a half-moon contour starting from above the breastbone (the bit where they begin to swell) and going over the top, sweeping out towards your underarm. The secret is to dust lightly and blend well, otherwise your secret will be well and truly exposed! Another beauty tip is to give your breasts the 'wow' factor by applying a skin-tinted shimmer between your cleavage. It tricks the eye into thinking your breasts are actually plumper than they are.

Pray for a better pair

Praying for a bigger bust might actually work! To strengthen the muscles that support your boobs, adopting a prayer position is one exercise personal trainers recommend. Place the palms of your hands together so that they're in a prayer position, and press them together straight in front of your chest so that your elbows jut out at right angles. As your muscles contract and get to work, feel your breasts magically lift. Repeat up to 25 times a day.

> ### LIFE-LONG TIP
> ★ *If you desire a fuller pair and want to boost your cup size, shop clever. Seek out chicken-fillet breast enhancers you can slip into your bra. They're comfortable, have no health risks and mould to your body, giving a sexy, natural shape. A wrapover top or dress that willingly pushes your breasts together is a great cheat too.*

A life lesson in holiday glamour

Yippee! It's summer and the holiday living should be easy. But life is a beach and holiday chic can be pretty hard to master where seasonal problems can kick off from the moment you take off – whether you're flying first, club or cattle class! From acting like you're part of the St Tropez jet set to looking luscious on landing and dressing up in relaxed style, follow these tips for being vacation happy.

Take off looking first-class gorgeous

First off: nail the art of looking airport-chic. A word of warning: you want to feel comfortable but not look too comfortable. So ditch the tracksuit. The best terminal dressers look carefree-comfy as well as chic, so go for the smart-casual look of jeans worn with flat shoes such as ballet pumps teamed with finely woven cotton T-shirts that can be layered over one another and then unlayered if you get too hot. Hitting the check-in looking chic, calm and collected also ups your chances of being upgraded. Wear a pair of large shades, too – they always look glam.

Make the most of your air time

Forget the in-flight entertainment, if you want to look terrific on touchdown you need to get pampering. Once seated, remove all your make-up; not only will you feel fresher but also if you do happen to doze off you won't wake up with panda eyes. Take disposable wipes that cleanse and moisturise with one nifty sweep. Follow with a self-tanning moisturiser so that you arrive looking healthy, and combat hydration by regularly spritzing with a moisture mist. Apply make-up just before landing – a creamy pink across the lips and cheeks gives pooped skin a pep up. For long-haul hairdressing, take a reviving mist and spray to restyle a flat hairdo. Drink copious amounts of water, avoid the caffeine and stodge in your meal (eat the fruit and protein) and wiggle your ankles to combat fluid retention and puffiness.

Do some blue-sky thinking

I always envy women who can throw together a holiday wardrobe without packing absolutely everything. Make no mistake, it's an art form and takes confidence, but it's a skill that can be mastered. I never bother with trousers (except when flying) when going on a beach-bound holiday, as it's usually too sizzling to wear them. For a holiday minus the fashion hassles here's a quick getaway list:

- **Pretty cotton dresses** You can dress them down for sightseeing worn with flip-flops and a wide-brimmed floppy sunhat, or dress them up for after hours with sling-backs, an armful of bracelets, a pair of bold earrings or a statement-style necklace.

- **Figure-skimming tops** You can never take too many. Roll up and stuff them in your holdall, as they can be worn with sarongs and skirts, and over bikinis.

- **Kaftans** They can double up not only as beachwear but also as stylish cover-ups in the evening.

- **Shorts/denim cut-offs** They look sexy. Wear with a belt slung low on the hips.

- **Swimwear** Pack lots! It's your main fashion reason for

taking to the skies. Plus, bikini tops look sassy when worn with shorts or skirts.

- **Bags** Pack a large and roomy beach bag for day and a clutch bag for bar hopping.

- **Shoes** Take flip-flops as well as a pair of more dressy sandals. Just make sure you wear them with a polished pedicure.

- **Sunglasses** These are your mainstay, not only for warding off wrinkles – squinting in the sun is the fastest route to crow's feet – but they can also be used as a hairband and, most importantly, make you look cool and mysterious.

- **Jewellery** Don't take your expensive stuff away, instead seek out local buys and throw them together like a local!

LIFE-LONG TIP

Lower your risk of deep-vein thrombosis (DVT) by taking the supplement pycnogenol. A pine bark extract, it's renowned for its ability to support blood vessels, reinforcing capillary walls and ensuring normal blood flow. Take two capsules daily up to a week before your flight.

A life lesson in everyday amazing hair

Ultimately, hair is a reflection of our youth, vitality, health and fertility, and contributes to our feeling of gorgeousness enormously. It's also deeply sexual – anthropologists believe the way you choose to wear your hair and play with it acts as a form of foreplay. It is also seen as a social barometer where the state of your hair (shiny, swingy and sexy) can sway your relationships and career for the better. If you've had enough bad hair days to last a lifetime, isn't it about time you addressed the mane issues?

Don't be afraid to divorce your hairdresser

It's a no-brainer: if you don't love your hairdresser, you're not gonna love your hair. I can't emphasise how important it is to click with your stylist. It's a relationship much like a marriage that's based on trustworthiness and dependability with a little bit of excitement thrown in. Your cut is the biggest deal-breaker of the lot when it comes to amazing hair, and if your hairdresser has lost interest it's time to move on. Your hairstyle should be constantly evolving, even if it's just a few snipped-in layers, a couple of centimetres or so shorter or a tweak with the colour, otherwise you risk being stuck in the land hair forgot. If your stylist doesn't look pleased to see you, or handles your hair like he's tossing a limp salad then that awkward conversation needs to come up where you say, 'We've been together a long time and I think it's time for me (and my hair) to move on.' Why stick with never being satisfied with your hair because you can't bring yourself to dump your stylist?

Fill up your follicles

Make no mistake, low-fat diets spell out disaster for your tresses. If the body is deprived of life-enhancing nutrients, such as good fats found in olive oil, fatty acids and omega-3 sourced in fish and nuts, it will rob them from our hair (and nails), which are seen as non-vital for survival. The upshot? Without valuable nutrients such as the B vitamins and sufficient iron and zinc, healthy hair growth just won't happen. Find the B vitamins in wholegrains, brown rice and pulses; iron in fortified breakfast cereals, leafy green veg and meat; and zinc in pumpkin seeds and Brazil nuts. Some studies have linked hair loss – also seen in women – with a lowered capability to tolerate sugar. This pre-diabetic condition has been branded as Syndrome X, where the solution is to steer clear of refined sugar and excite your taste buds with fresh and dried fruit instead. And since hair is a protein it makes sense to treat like with like, so look to feasting on turkey and eggs! Another great hair booster is silica (take in supplement form), which is necessary for the rebuilding of all connective tissue, including hair. It's said to speed up hair growth and thickness.

Get on the best-tressed list

Grabbing the hair you want not only comes down to having a genius cut but also to the products and appliances you are using. A shampoo bespoke for your hair type is paramount – find a couple of good ones and alternate. Intensive conditioning is heaven to a mop of hair that's constantly subjected to heat abuse, so do this at least twice a week. Keep products to a minimum, otherwise hair winds up acting lifeless through build-up. Generally, a thickening spray used on the roots gives hair movement, a heat protector for those that are addicted to straightening irons or tongs prevents dehydration and a serum or wax for a glass-like gleam is enough. A natural barrel bristle brush is the answer for smooth, bouncy styles, or those who prefer their locks straight and sleek should go for a paddle brush, which glides through the hair. For straightening irons, make sure they're ceramic, as they help lock in moisture, and for dryers look for the word 'ionic': they dry hair faster and break down moisture with very little heat.

Sex up your hair

Don't let your hair hang around doing nothing, experiment with it and double your sex appeal at the same time. Tousled hair always looks great, so work in a little mousse and roughly blow-dry. A ponytail nestled at the nape of the neck with a little teasing on the crown makes you look sexily flirty and showcases a long neck something wonderful. For a glam up-do, sweep half your hair up while keeping the rest down. And a fringe that's swept to the side and falls teasingly over the eye gives you a certain sexual knowingness. Colour can really vamp up your hair, too. But talk to your colourist about the upkeep of your hue before getting gowned up. Ask how often you need to visit the salon (with a solid colour roots will show quickly). If you're cash strapped, opt for highlights that are low maintenance. In between visits revive colour at home with colour-infused shampoos and conditioners.

LIFE-LONG TIP

★ *Don't book an appointment with your stylist first thing on a Monday morning. You don't want a 'hungover' haircut!*

A life lesson in (naturally) great performing skin

The science of how skin ages and performs has come a long way since the invention of cold cream. No longer do we have to age gracefully – high-tech creams take care of that (they don't even have to be expensive). And we don't need to go under the knife for a wind-in-the-tunnel like mask, because, thanks to more know-how, it's becoming easier than ever to turn into your own super-facialist.

Give skin a clean break

According to experts, skin has become ever grubbier thanks to the environment becoming dirtier. For skin to be able to function properly, and therefore to look its gleaming best, layers of pollution, long-lasting make-up and the skin's own sebum initially need to be removed in order for those expensive products you splashed out on to work at their optimum. It's been reported that the majority of women still use soap to wash away the day's grime, but bear in mind that soap is from the same family as detergents, so you may as well be washing your face with bathroom cleaner! As with everything, time and attention get the best results, but with 20 seconds being the average time that women spend cleansing that's not saying

18

much for our skin hygiene. The newest thinking on getting skin super-clean is the 'double cleansing' technique, which provides a deeper, more thorough cleanse and the use of a pre-cleansing oil. A new must-have in skincare, a lightweight oil is used first to melt surface debris, which is then followed up by your normal cleanser. The result? Skin perfection at your fingertips.

Discover skin-changing ingredients

Skin therapists dictate that we have arrived in an era where skin is no longer classified by age, but has become a true product of our lifestyles. So, it goes without saying that too much of the (bad) feel-good stuff such as alcohol, cigarettes and sun do nothing good for the condition of your skin. Stress and the environment are increasingly adding to skin hassles such as adult acne and psoriasis, so the research into sourcing potent antioxidants, which act like a police force for the skin, has become ever more important. Over 100 antioxidants have been discovered in the past 15 years and new ones are constantly being developed. Far from looking out for common antioxidants such as A, C and E when scanning for skin-solving ingredients, start to search for these specialist antioxidants on the ingredient list such as green and white tea, idebenone, fennel seed extract and grape seed extract, all of which help keep skin strong and keep free radicals at bay. Enzymes are big news, too, as they help resurface the skin for a smoother looking complexion. Look for a mask and apply twice a week.

Listen to what your skin is telling you

Whether your main concern is smoothness, a more even tone or getting your hands on the latest hi-tech creams, there is an answer on a shelf near you. It's just finding it. But, first off, it's crucial to listen to what your skin is telling you. It's called psycho-dermatology where the state of your mind profoundly affects the state of your skin. If you're stressed, you harvest a crop of spots and your skin is lacklustre. When you're happy, you glow, baby! Remember: sometimes it's your lifestyle that needs to be addressed rather than adding another layer of cream.

Slough to smooth

One of the biggest breakthroughs for at-home dermatology has been microdermabrasion kits: superior types of exfoliators boasting abrasives you can buy off the shelf. In short: they're a shortcut to better-looking skin. The power of microdermabrasion is its ability to allow more even-toned, younger-looking skin to form by using controlled 'sanding'. A build-up of dead skin cells adds up to lifeless-looking skin and a loss of radiance. Once cleared, the surface is retexturised and the skin literally sees a new dawn where the complexion takes on a new awakening. Carry out twice a week and use a moisturiser with an SPF15 to protect freshly scrubbed skin.

LIFE-LONG TIP
★ *Make it with the lava lamp and learn to meditate. If you don't worry about wrinkles, chances are you won't have to deal with them!*

A life lesson in beauty's little essentials

When it comes to looking constantly good, every girl has to double up as a secret agent and bag a handful of beauty weapons. Here is a checklist of everyday, desert-island essentials that should make it on your most-wanted list.

Adopt foundation intelligence

A radiant complexion is never out of fashion and the right base is key to a flawless complexion. Whatever make-up look you're road testing, it all starts with great skin. First up: assess your skin type. For dry skin opt for moisture-rich foundations, for oily skin it's a no-brainer to choose an oil-free formulation, and for more mature skins go for a treatment-based foundation with added vitamins to minimise fine lines. Build a foundation wardrobe, too: skin changes seasonally so may require a more nurturing formula in the winter. Obviously, skin tone will be lighter in the winter and darker in the summer so a colour switch adds up to a more natural look. Have an 'emergency' foundation for an SOS (save-our-skin) call-out. An illuminating anti-fatigue foundation that contains pigments to disguise shadows is a skin saver for partied-out complexions the next morning.

Cover clever with concealer

For an even-toned complexion, concealer is your answer. A creamy easy-to-blend concealer is the universal solution to covering dark circles around the eyes and any redness around the nose. Dab and blend sparingly. Alternatively, look for brightening pens that brighten dark shadows and minimise discolouration.

Flash and reveal those lashes

Mascara is one precious eye reviver. Even if you haven't got time to sweep on shadow, a flick of true black mascara will magnify lashes and open up slept-in eyes like nothing else. Choose a smudgeproof formula and look for a thick brush to boost up lashes with rich, dense colour. Don't forget to apply mascara to the outer lashes too as they really give a 'kick' to the eye.

Become a cheeky girl

There's nothing like a spot of blush therapy. A healthy glow flushed onto the apples of your cheeks acts as an instant radiance boost. Opt for shades that flatter and seamlessly blend with your own natural colouring. Don't skimp on pots either. Buy two shades: one that mimics the colour of your cheeks when naturally flushed (notice the hue post-love making!) and a brighter colour to make your whole look jump and provide more of a fashion statement. A bronzing powder is an alternative for the I've-just-been-on-a-fabulous-holiday glow when brushed across the cheeks and bridge of the nose.

Colour and gloss your lips

Lips, when polished and groomed with a slick of gloss or a swipe of lipstick, immediately bring your look together. And it is one of the easiest ways to update your style and give an edge to your make-up. Like foundation, build up a wardrobe of colours that you can then custom-blend however and whenever you please. Lip tints give an ultra-high shine gloss, giving lips a fruity punch, and are easy to use on the go, whereas a creamy, semi-matte lipstick gives a couture-like finish to lips, thanks to its full coverage. Bold colours take confidence to wear, but once worn, are never forgotten! If wearing a strong red, blot the colour down with a tissue or a dusting of translucent powder for a modern texture. Lip balm should always be a beauty essential, too. Chapped lips never get kissed.

LIFE-LONG TIP

★ *No self-respecting beauty agent should be without a slanted pair of tweezers. Not only essential for grooming unruly brows, they're also indispensable for dealing with troublesome lonesome hairs found sprouting in unladylike places – the corner of the upper lip for instance.*

CHAPTER 2
Style, Slingbacks and Stealing the Spotlight

A life lesson in buying and looking sexy in a bikini

Unless you've graced the cover of a magazine, bikini shopping has the seasonal habit of sending us all into an insecure frenzy. The perfect bikini can make your summer – you can pose for every picture without feeling self-conscious – the secret is in the shopping and in adjusting your attitude.

Make like a cover girl

Buying a bikini is a baring experience. You're practically naked in the changing room illuminated, more often than not, with harsh lighting. And, let's face it, most of us will go shopping for a bikini before our holiday, so pasty, bumpy skin does little to crank up much-needed body confidence. So, before you hit the changing rooms aim to spend a little time beautifying a body that has been hidden under winter layers. First up: exfoliate to rid a build-up of dry skin cells; start from the feet upwards, paying attention to knees and elbows. Next, slather your body daily with a hardworking lotion. Modern formulations help tackle anything from lack of firmness to uneven pigmentation. Then, self-tan like a pro for a quick, even,

I-look-great glow. It does wonders for minimising flaws and gives the illusion of making you look at least 2.25kg (5lb) slimmer.

Go undercover

Trying on a bikini can be a very intimate experience for many of us, so if you're feeling a little shy, hunt out boutique-like stores with individual dressing rooms rather than a gawp-for-all communal changing area. Although the selection might be smaller, the lighting is usually kinder and you can at least take your time looking in the mirror in the safety of your cubical – without feeling self-conscious and pondering whether the bikini(s) make your butt look big. And don't forget to wear tight-fitting underwear so that you can slip bikinis on without lots of unnecessary bulging and padding.

Don't get hung up about your size

A bikini is worn to flaunt your womanly curves. Unless you're naturally skinny, you're going to have a belly, hips and breasts. Don't fret about them, learn to love them. Think Bridget Bardot and Ursula Andress in the 1960s (rent *Dr No* for reference and inspiration), where the bikini fashion emphasis was rounded, sophisticated and incredibly sexy. Leave the beach with onlookers shaken and stirred!

Expect the unexpected

Be prepared to try on lots of different styles of bikinis to find the perfect one. Like everything else, you can easily get stuck in a rut and find yourself not moving on from a cut you've been wearing for years. A pear shape, for instance, may never have thought of trying on a string bikini, as you're probably used to wearing big pants (which only make your bottom look bigger), but a tie-to-fit bikini bottom works marvels to balance out the load. With strings you can tie them tight enough so that pants stay up, but loose enough so that they don't cut into the hips. Move the strings up to your hips, too, and see how you create an instant V-shape, slendering down your troublesome lower half.

If all else fails buy a swimsuit

Don't feel a failure if you really can't find a bikini that flatters and makes you want to strut your funky stuff down the boardwalk. Some of the sexiest sights on the beach are women wearing a one-piece. The secret with swimsuits is that you can choose what to peek-a-boo! Depending on where they're cutaway, you can choose which of your assets to flaunt and which to keep hidden. Generally, many one-pieces will cover the tummy and show more back, you can then opt for a style that's either cut deep at the front to flaunt some cleavage or cut high on the thigh to show off your legs.

LIFE-LONG TIP

Get into the habit of mixing and matching your bikini separates. Marry a polka dot top with a striped bottom for instance. It's fun and makes for an original look – just remember dark hues work great at the beginning of your hols, whereas wearing tropical shades in the second half of your holiday will max your tan. These bright and zingy colours will make your tan look more sun kissed.

A life lesson in being a jean genius

Where would a girl be without her denims? It's said that happiness can be found in the perfect pair of jeans – and I don't doubt that! A pair of sexy denims is really a wardrobe wonder where they can look cool, retro or chic. Ultimately they can rock your look, give you instant style status as well as slim the hips and lengthen the legs. Here's a spot of jean therapy to make your blues work for you.

Inherit the jean gene

Buying jeans can be put on a similar par to buying a bikini: when you get it right, you look and feel like a million dollars. But when you get it wrong you feel like throwing yourself into the bargain bucket. Jeans can also be likened to guys: you have to shop around and try a lot on until you find your match made in heaven. Get into the habit of trying on jeans, even if you haven't specifically gone out to nail down a pair. Jean shopping can be lengthy and tiresome as there are so many cuts and brands, but the more you try on in passing the better you'll get at judging which styles suit you at first glance. And once you've found a perfect cut, stockpile them. There's nothing more irritating when you go back to buy another pair than finding they've discontinued your cut.

Know your bootleg from your skinny leg

The cut of your jean leg is crucial for making the most of your legs. The bootleg cut is the most flattering to most body shapes. By staying fitted on the thighs and then flaring out slightly at the end of the jean the bootcut will usually slenderise generous hips or bottoms and lengthen with its more generous cut on the lower leg. They look great when worn with heels – just make sure you get the length right. The longer the hem, the longer your legs will look. Jeans should never rest on top of the shoe, but graze at least down to half the heel. Skinny jeans go in and out of fashion, but are best suited to a boyish figure as they are unforgiving. Worn mostly by indie chicks, they work well with flats. If you've got big feet, then this style probably isn't for you, as you will wind up looking like a penguin – and, unlike the bootcut, the length should fall shorter onto the shoe. For those who like the idea of the skinny cut, but aren't built like a beanpole, opt for a straight leg.

Get the waist right

There's nothing worse than a pair of jeans that are too tight on the waist, resulting in a spilling over of flesh. Generally speaking, mid- to low-waisted jeans are the most flattering. They sit lower on the hips, which adds up to making your torso look instantly longer as well as slimmer. Great if you're feeling a little bit 'stomachy', as they draw the eye away from the midriff zone. Just be aware that this cut can visually shorten the leg, so buy them long. High-waisted jeans have an on-and-off love affair with the fashion set. Only wear them if you have the figure of a rake.

Handpick your pockets

Pockets are the finishing touches on jeans but need attention paid to them. Points to keep in mind are: the smaller the pocket, the bigger your butt will look. Ditto flaps on pockets. If pockets are slung too low on the bum, they will make your bottom look saggy, not pert. The most flattering of pockets should be slightly turned outwards for a perkier looking bottom.

Watch your wash

Denim comes in many shades of blue – just use the fading to your advantage. Darker coloured denims are obviously more slimming than a washed-out blue, and a darker rinse along the inner thighs will also magically create the illusion of slimmer legs.

LIFE-LONG TIP

If your weight tends to go up and down, then opt for a pair of jeans that offer a little stretch. This way you can pack on a few pounds and still be able to wriggle into your favourite pair.

A life lesson in turning heads at a party

What girl can't say it's a great feeling when she has the magnetic power to swivel heads around in a room? Celebrities get double takes because of their status, but for us mere mortals it takes a little more effort to get that wow-look-at-her moment. Here's how to crack the attention code on being your very own 'it' girl.

Go the extra mile

Now, this may sound obvious, but if you don't dress up and make an effort, how can you be expected to make a lasting impression on anybody? I've been to parties where girls have turned up looking like they've just left the stables after mucking out the horses. And then wonder why nobody has asked them to dance, offered them a drink or a lift home. It's a self-sabotaging move thinking that just your wit and joie de vivre will carry you glamorously through the evening. Of course everybody loves a girl who's good for a laugh – but you don't want the laugh to be on you! If you're walking into a room full of strangers who are inevitably going to make instant judgements about you, your dress sense and the way you've put yourself together count.

To get down to basics: firstly, wash and fragrance your hair. There's nothing more confidence boosting than wafting about with gorgeous-smelling, well-performing hair. Secondly, never wear anything baggy. Oversized clothes shrink your presence. Whatever your size, wear something that hugs your curves and makes you feel special. This way you will move and act more confidently. And lastly, wear or do something that someone will notice and comment on. It could be the way you've applied your make-up, the wearing of a gorgeous necklace or the way in which you've styled your hair.

Boost your body language

There's little point in wearing a jaw-dropping dress if your body language shouts 'stay away'. Well-behaved flirting and a natural, friendly smile are very sexy and attract men like bees to the proverbial honey pot. A girl that maximises her girlishness will always turn heads, as it throws out a fun and playful spirit that makes you look relaxed. If it's a certain man you want to make an impression on, you don't even have to be overtly sexual – in fact, too brash behaviour can put men off. Instead, make bold eye contact, smile and slowly walk over to him. Put a little sway into your hips, too – a swagger never did a girl any harm! Make your body language welcoming by opening up your arms and touching him gently on the forearm, and lean in towards him to introduce yourself. Trust me, he will be completely mesmerised.

Reveal something about yourself

… but not too much. Sharing a small intimacy – such as the music you like, or the type of holiday you've just come back from – encourages a confidence-à-deux without getting initially too close. In the tell-it-all-reality-television world we live in now, it's all too easy to reveal in the first five minutes your tragic dating history or your recurring skin problem! This is getting comfortable far too fast and will more than likely send the man you want to hook and reel in scurrying. You will turn heads and keep them turned (and interested) if you hold back on your Oprah moments.

Act fabulous!

A girl who wears her insecurities like a badge of honour will always be looking at the backs of heads! If you're constantly asking 'does my bum look big in this?' or generally putting yourself down, it pushes people into complimenting you.

Ideally, a compliment should always come voluntarily. Although it may take a lot of bravado, acting sexually confident will make you come across as electrifying, not needy. Ultimately, the right amount of sexual va-va-voom can turn a wallflower into a siren.

LIFE-LONG TIP

★ Role reverse and give the man you fancy a great big compliment. You'll be remembered just for being unconventional.

A life lesson in buying bags and sunglasses

Like shoes, bags and sunglasses have quickly become the Holy Grail when talking about accessories. They can also be the two things that inject fashion fuel into an otherwise dressed-down outfit, which is why I've dedicated these pages to talking about these two life-enhancing fashion trimmings.

Make it a must-have bag

All my girlfriends have turned into crazy bag ladies. In fact it's got rather competitive. Bags used to be items that you just blindly stuffed all your necessaries into, now they're a major fashion item in their own right. The ultra-expensive designer ones are even known by names. Like a new pair of shoes, a new bag can really update and add punch to your outfit, but apart from it looking good, what else should you consider when buying? Well, you should always try it on. This may sound silly, but a bag has to flatter and work with your build. If it's too big it will swamp you and look ridiculous. Likewise, a small bag can make a bigger girl look, well, bigger.

A girl that wants to take attention away from her hips should opt for a bag that nestles snugly under her arm rather than one with a long strap that hits the biggest part of her.

To get it right, slip the bag over your shoulder and study yourself from all angles. Other considerations to make are: is it roomy enough? If a bag is stuffed to the max and looks fit to burst, it ruins the shape of it to the point where you might as well be carrying an old carrier bag. If you can't fit everything into your bag why not carry two? A shoulder bag for keys, mobile and money, and an extra – but equally nice – hand-held bag for all your other bits and pieces. It makes for double the compliments!

Another thing you should always check is: does the bag comfortably fit you? A bag with a shortish strap may not slip comfortably over your shoulder when wearing a winter coat, for example. And finally, is it worth your hard-earned cash? Bags that shout for your full attention can cost a small fortune, and although they should be of the highest quality, some of them sadly aren't. If you decide to buy one such bag, tug at the handles before buying it to make sure they're strong, check the seams and make sure the stitching isn't split and runs even. Run the zip up and down a couple of times, too, checking that it works smoothly. And inspect the leather. Will it stand the test of time when used most days?

Looking cool in shades

Sunglasses are cool for many reasons. Firstly, they make anybody look famous. Secondly, they protect your eyes from the sun (which is why they were initially first invented), thirdly they disguise bleary eyes, and lastly they ward off crow's feet – all that squinting is very ageing. Like bags, it pays to build up a wardrobe of sunglasses so that you can mix 'n' match them with your outfits. But the first step is not to follow fashion blindly (excuse the pun). Like a great haircut, a great-looking pair of sunnies needs to flatter your face shape. The following tips will help:

- **Heart shaped** This is a cute-looking face with high cheek-bones and a small, dainty chin. For this reason don't make your sunglasses overly big or you will look like a bug. Angular ones will show off cheekbones as well as helping to balance out and soften the face.

- **Round** This face shape always looks young (lucky you), where the width is equal to the length. With this in mind don't wear huge, round sunglasses – they will make your face look like a moon. Cat-eyed shapes will reduce plump-ness and give the illusion of elongating the face. Deep colours such as browns and reds give a sophisticated edge.

- **Oval** Most styles of sunglasses will suit, as you have a balanced face with enviably high cheekbones. In this case you can afford to go for bold shapes such as square ones.

- **Square** This face shape can look quite angular with a wide chin and forehead. Curved and oval shapes will help soften the face while lengthening. Avoid rectangular frames, which will only highlight angles on your face.

> ### LIFE-LONG TIP
> ★ *Give your bag the love you give your shoes. Look after the leather by polishing it and spray-guarding it against rain. As for sunglasses, keep them in a case when not wearing them. Scratched lenses are annoying and very preventable.*

A life lesson in shopping for fabulous shoes

Whether they're flat, wedged or super-high, shoes are one of life's reasons for living. The trick is to find a pair that puts you a step ahead of fashion without hobbling and limping around in pain.

Don't be a mean girl to your feet

Shopping for shoes can be likened to walking into a candy store. You want them all and blow the consequences. In terms of sweets, it's bigger hips. In terms of shoes, it's squashed toes and the risk of corns. By acting like one of the ugly sisters in Cinderella and trying to push your foot into an ill-fitting shoe in the hope that it will stretch out won't do your feet any favours at all. At least 85 per cent of women wear shoes that are the wrong size. With this in mind get your feet measured professionally. You probably haven't had this done since you were a kid, but as we age, feet get larger (especially after pregnancy) and you may find you've gone up a size. Wearing a bigger size can actually make your foot look more streamlined instead of bunched up. Always shop for shoes in the afternoon when your feet are more swollen. And don't just slip them on, move around in them. Besides a few little steps, wiggle and stretch out your toes, and rotate your ankles. If the shoes feel tight or rub in any way, perhaps go up half a size.

43

Seek out foot therapy

A gorgeous pair of shoes – which are rarely sensible – work as an instant fashion fix with the risk of ruining your feet and putting out your back. Therefore it's a trend that is not universally loved by foot experts. But their age-old advice of wearing shoes to resemble that of a policewoman just doesn't cut the mustard with the modern girl. Instead, my listen-to-me advice is to book your feet in with a podiatrist every few months. Although not pampering – not a bottle of polish is in sight – they do indeed sort out your feet. These professionals are licensed to use scary-looking scalpels to scrap off unsightly callused skin and dig out those in-between-your-toes corns that can otherwise feel like they are crippling you. They also train their keen foot-fetish eyes on spotting early signs of trouble such as an in-growing toenail, nail fungus or the beginnings of a bunion – not foot accessories a girl likes to boast about.

Work out your feet

Kick off your shoes as soon as you walk through the door at home and potter around barefoot to stretch them out. After bathing, take five minutes each night to massage them. Raise them on a pillow, grip your toes and pull the foot towards your chest. It works like Pilates for the foot. Take time out to massage the balls of your feet, too. Massaging will help plump up this much-put-upon area like a cushion – it gets all the hammering caused by stilettos having pitched your weight forward.

Walk like a diva (not an Egyptian!)

Accidents can occur when wearing heels. Ankles can be broken, knees can be grazed, and it goes without saying your pride also takes a fall. The Society of Chiropodists and Podiatrists – who have your feet's best interests at heart – recommend 'gliding' to minimise damage to your feet. They advocate not looking as if you're rushing for a bus, but slowing down, taking ladylike steps and shortening your stride when wearing heels. When it comes to technique, their well-heeled advice is to put your heel down first and then glide. This is especially true when wearing slingbacks, which never look princess-like if clomped around in.

> ### *LIFE-LONG TIP*
> ★ *Wear heels when supermarket shopping. You can reach items on high shelves. Otherwise, try to wear different shoes each day, varying the styles and height of the heel. This will stop your feet from hitting the ground in the same way and help prevent your Achilles tendons from shortening and your calf and ankle muscles from over-tightening.*

A life lesson in avoiding a fashion faux pas

Let's get two points straight: there are fashion fashionistas (girls that are in the know when it comes to hemlines, colours and styles and throw the whole lot together effortlessly) and then there are fashion victims (girls that wind up wearing every trend going – whether it flatters them or not – and come across looking slightly gaga). Here's how to mimic the former.

Surf the trends ... but wear them only if they suit you

The key to not ending up a victim of high fashion is working out what suits you. If you can't get your head around this, then fashion will always be your foe rather than your friend. When drooling over looks straight from the catwalk, remember: it's from a fashion show. Yes, that word 'show' might give you a clue why even gazelle-like models can look totally ridiculous when trussed up in some of the clownish creations. When in the changing room coveting fashion's hot new looks, a simple trick is to ask yourself, 'Does it suit me?' rather than, 'Is it in fashion?' Aim for that overused word 'style' and you will (I hope) not be taken hostage with an unsuitable look.

It's not always about the new

It seems that sometimes fashion was created to make us feel insecure. So therefore we spend, spend, spend to feel better about ourselves and keep up with fellow clotheshorses. It gets to the point where we're frightened to put on a black polo neck unless some fashion expert from the television has said it's OK with them. Relax. Fashion victims are never relaxed, which is why they become them. It's a bit like the Emperor's New Clothes: don't believe all you see or hear. So-called seasonal fashion 'must-haves' always tend to be over the top: bubble skirts, platforms, the colour yellow (which never suits anyone except for redheads, where it can look rather good!). The answer? Just say 'no'. Women with style know what suits them and wear a variation on a much-loved, always-works-for-me theme. It's all about being fashionably on top.

Reign in your inner Pollyanna

Don't wear everything at once. Being a real life walking, talking mannequin doll shouldn't be a look one should seek to copy. If the Western look is in, for example, don't feel tempted to wear the Stetson, the cowboy boots, the chaps and the poncho. Just try wearing a pair of slim-fitting jeans with a gorgeous silver-buckled belt teamed with a shirt, for example. There's no need to go the whole Dolly Parton route to get your fashion point across.

Personalise (not penalise) your look

Go ahead and buy strong statement pieces – but then work out how to make them your own. You want to look like you're 'in-the-know' not a 'no-hoper'. Let these freshly added-to-your-wardrobe pieces shine by all means, but play down the rest of your look with some of your old favourites.

> ### *LIFE-LONG TIP*
> ★ *Think of high fashion as a one-night stand with a guy you feel slightly embarrassed about the next morning. And style as a long and passionate affair that you want to go on forever.*

CHAPTER 3
(Home) Comfort, Cushions and Clutter

A life lesson in finding a happy home

It isn't only Dorothy in *The Wizard of Oz* who believes there's no place like home. Your home – whether you own it or rent it – should act as a calming sanctuary away from all the madness of the outside world, bringing harmony and comfort as well as energy. Here are pointers for finding the perfect nest.

It's all about location

I don't want to sound like an estate agent here, but location is important. If you find yourself in an area that makes you feel down in the dumps every time you step out of your own front door, then it's not going to be a great property love-in. Remember: you can change almost anything about your place, but you cannot change the area it's in.

Before home hunting, make a list of what's important to you. Do you need to be within walking distance of a tube line or a railway station? If so, how far are you prepared to walk? A half-hour walk in the summer might seem great, but how would you feel in the winter? How noisy is the road you will be living on? Open the windows and check out the surround sound. The same goes if it's near a school. Great if you don't mind the sound of kids, but hell if you do. What does the high street offer? Does it have a cluster of nice coffee shops, a good newsagent and a shop where you can pop out to get a pint of milk and a loaf of bread after 8.00 p.m.?

It doesn't matter what's on your checklist, if it's important to you, then it matters. I know someone who always checks out if there's somewhere she can pop in for a quick sunbed session before she even considers changing her door number.

Is there a room with a view?

Beyond location, the next thing to look at is the details about your actual home. Consider things beyond room size and whether you like the colour of the front door. For example, what's the light quality like in the rooms? A basement flat with very little light streaming through can get pretty depressing very quickly. Think what the rooms will look like on a dark, rainy day. Do you have views? Again resting your eye on a scene you like is important. Sitting in your living room and looking directly into a launderette with people washing their smalls may not be your idea of relaxing downtime. Check out your privacy, too. Who are you overlooked by, do you feel comfortable with it? Having to sneak about in your own home to avoid prying eyes does not make for happy nesting.

Spy on your neighbours

Bad neighbours are not to be recommended. You could be living in your dream home, but if you've got troublesome company next door you're never going to feel totally relaxed. When checking out properties generally, ask what the neighbours are like. Obviously, if they cause trouble then you won't be told, but the clues are there! Is there a recycling box filled to the brim with wine and beer bottles? If so, they probably party hard and you could be in for some sleepless nights. Do they keep their gardens tidy or are they a rubbish tip? If you share a pathway, you don't really want to be tripping over other people's trash. Do they have big, barking dogs? If so, perhaps it's a sign you should look elsewhere!

Consider your lifestyle

To be truly kick-your-shoes-off happy, your home needs to reflect your personality and who you are. If you're into vintage and get pleasure from looking at old fireplaces then a modern-style flat is going to leave you feeling unsatisfied. Likewise, if you can't stand over-the-top decorative fuss then a Victorian property full of mouldings and swirls is going to do your head in. Look at the features as you 'shop' and consider if you could live with them. Think in practical terms, too. Do you really need three bedrooms and two bathrooms if you live alone? A large home can feel luxurious, but remember: the extra space adds up to buying more furniture and gives you bigger heating bills. Alternatively, you can get a lodger or flatmate, which can help with your outgoings.

LIFE-LONG TIP

When 'shopping' for new accommodation always be nice to the owners or landlords. You'll be surprised how many don't sell or rent to people whom they take an instant dislike to.

A life lesson in cleaning your place in an hour

The trouble with cleaning is it's deeply psychological: the actual thought of doing it is so much worse than actually rolling up your sleeves and getting on with it. The answer is: do a speed-clean. That's cleaning without seemingly having to put too much effort into it. The results? You'll feel in control, have more time for the things you like doing and you won't have to pretend to be out when a drop-in guest bangs on the door, for fear of vicious gossip that you've turned into a hobo. Read on for clever domestic shortcuts.

Clear the decks

I always look at the hallway like a ship's deck: it's the first impression you have of the place. A crowded hallway where you step over rows of shoes and kick your way through bags makes you feel irritated before you even reach the cabin. Survey the scene and deal with it appropriately. That's putting away shoes, hanging up coats and bags, and throwing away flyers (which seem to plop through the letterbox every two seconds).

Pick that skirt off the floor

Put this into the 'I must obey the one-minute rule' category, which rolls on all week. This means if the chore takes less than one minute – whether it's picking up an item of clothing, rinsing up a cup or throwing away yesterday's paper – then do it. This minute. Trust me, it's an instant solution for avoiding piles of mess at the end of the week.

Focus on clutter and rubbish

First off, tackle all your stacks. That's stacks of anything: magazines, dirty laundry, dishes … and deal with them – even if it means stacking them out of sight. Then clear all the table tops – it makes your room look bigger and brings calm. Now for the rubbish. Rubbish isn't only the binning of last night's takeaway (which should be in the one-minute-rule category), but anything that's not obviously useful or decorative. This task should be limited to what you can see and should take only about 10 minutes.

Make your bed

Along with plumping up cushions and putting out clean towels in the bathroom, this is the one chore that can be done in a millisecond and it really pulls the room together. Beat the pillows to create fullness and really shake the duvet. Not only is this good exercise for the arms and for ridding pent-up tension but it also has the magic of creating a wonderful hotel-like plumpness which makes falling into bed even more of a pleasure.

Dust bust

A layer of dust makes the place look dingy, unloved and fusty. The secret to dusting is letting gravity do the work for you. Armed with a feather duster (they always look sexier than a cloth), tickle the dust until it drops down to the floor and then vacuum it up. This is the quickest and most efficient way to clean. If you're really strapped for time, simply speed-dust everything at eye level.

Get friendly with a lint roller

I can't recommend this nifty little cleaning tool enough – especially if you have pets. With one roll it will magically lift up stray hairs from sofas, chairs and lampshades.

Clean kitchen tops and sinks

A kitchen littered with unwashed crockery and a dirty sink isn't good for domestic karma. Pile everything into the dish-washer (or wash it up) and leave to air dry. Next, wipe over bacteria-friendly spots such as work tops and handles. Then scrub the sink for all you're worth. Run round some bleach, then scrub with a sponge. Rinse well and admire the clean and white gleam. While donned up in rubber gloves, make your way to the bathroom. Spritz grime remover around the water line of the bath, scrub and rinse. Then bleach the loo.

Tackle the floors

If you have tiles on the bathroom and kitchen floors, a sharp spritz of all-purpose cleaner and a squeeze mop will do the trick without the need of a bucket of dirty water. For wooden floors sweep, and for carpets and rugs vacuum. If you've got a brush attachment, pop it on and run over the curtains and blinds.

LIFE-LONG TIP

★ *Clean your sink before you hit the pillow. Waking up to a dirty sink stacked with smelly crockery starts your day on the wrong foot. A clean sink will put a smile on your face in the morning.*

A life lesson in turning your bedroom into a (sensual) boudoir

Your bedroom should be looked upon as the 'soul' of your home, as it's a place you seek when the going gets rough and you want to retreat from a mad, bad world. Therefore, the decoration should invite pleasant and romantic thoughts. Here are some tips on making over your bedroom to enhance your mood as well as sexing up your relationship.

Create an atmosphere

All too often bedrooms are used as a dumping ground for dirty laundry and piles of ironing. Many don't even give you the headspace to relax, so with this in mind you owe it to yourself to turn it into a secret paradise and use purely for rest and romance. The first step is creating a mood that's different from your living room. A living room is where all the action goes on: television, chat, eating, entertaining … your bedroom should reflect the opposite. First, chuck out the television. A television steals away the room's peaceful vibe. It does nothing for your sex life either: a television is an energetic object that calls out to be turned on. The only thing you should think about switching on when in between the sheets is your man! Next, tidy up. Your bedroom is not meant to look like a launderette, office or gym. Buy a hamper and put in dirty clothes, find a cupboard to put in all your paperwork and tidy away dumbbells.

Now on to the lighting: it should be dim. Amber-coloured light is restful on the eyes and makes you look better naked. Forget about stark, overhead lighting and put your energies into searching for bedside lamps. Opt for richly coloured or patterned shades for an exotic feel. White shades can look too clinical and don't whip up enough atmosphere. Candles also work as a quick and easy mood enhancer. Buy a small armchair, too, for the corner of the room. It's great for intimate gossiping and makes discarded clothes look sexy, instead of sluttish when dumped on the floor!

Bedazzle your bed

A luxury-style love nest always comes down to the bed. It should be the focal point of the room and therefore make a statement. If you believe in the principles of feng shui, the most important thing is that you position the bed so that you are able to see the door to the room while lying in it. This is known as the 'power position'. If you have your back to the door, it creates a subconscious feeling of vulnerability. Make the bed look inviting. Keep it clear for a start. Nothing kills romance faster or makes you feel more exhausted than having to clear the top of the duvet of clutter before you even get under it.

Keep your bed linen good quality (always choose cotton over cotton mix, which makes you sweat) and unfussy. Men don't particularly get turned on by a bed adorned with over-the-top frills, but that's not to say you can't experiment with different-coloured duvet covers, blankets and cushions. Just make sure the fabrics are soft, sensuous and feel sexy on the skin – starchy wool blankets don't make for a cosy snuggle up. Change your bed linen once a week. No excuses. And iron your duvet cover. A bed should only look rumpled after lovemaking!

Give your furniture a facelift

Personally, I prefer bedroom furniture that you can move about and has character to it rather than a wall of fixed units. Shop around in junk shops for big beautiful wardrobes that make hanging your clothes in them an experience in itself. If you've got the room, treat yourself to a dressing table – it's the ultimate in bedroom pampering and makes getting ready all the more delightful. A full-length mirror whether free-standing or fixed onto the wall ensures you leave knowing what you look like from top to toe. Consider the pictures on your wall, too – do they inspire passion and love? The bedroom is one place you can hang sensual pictures without fear of your family seeing them. It's maybe wise to keep framed pictures of people other than your partner in a different room. There's nothing worse than being in the throes of passion with a line-up of your family looking at you!

LIFE-LONG TIP

Buy the biggest bed you can afford and one that fits proportionately into your room. It makes you feel safe and protected.

A life lesson in creating a heavenly lounge

Your living room is a place to kick off your shoes, lounge and relax. But, unlike your bedroom, it's open to a passing stream of human traffic. For this reason extra effort should be made to create an inviting, homely, comfortable and stylish all-welcome hang out.

The sofa: a one-stop comfort zone

Like a bed in a bedroom, a sofa in your living room is the place you automatically head for. But to get the most out of your sofa, there are fast and fixed rules you should think about before buying. The first is finding one that doesn't overwhelm the room. Yes, it's an important piece of furniture, but a common mistake is to pick one that dwarfs all the other features in the room – making it literally a sofa room, instead of a room that encourages free movement and flow. An over-sized sofa instantly gives the room a claustrophobic feel.

Once you've got the size mastered, colour and covering are the next things to consider. For this, consider your lifestyle. Do you have a baby, kids or pets? If so, then maybe cream or any other light-coloured fabric wouldn't be such a great choice. A fabric with a pattern works well as it has the knack of hiding dubious-looking stains. Beware of showroom seduction, too. It's so easy to be won over by materials such as suede, which look very cool and contemporary in the shop. Give yourself a reality check: how will it look after a year's time? Shiny, practically bald and littered with stains you just can't remove. Before you buy a sofa, ask for a fabric sample, take it home and pour some liquids and foods on it. Do they come out easily?

It's then on to the comfortability factor. When you find a style that you love, try it out. That means bouncing on it, lying down on it and more-or-less making sure it feels like a second bed. You don't want to perch on a sofa, you want to uncurl and loosen up on it.

Choose warm colours

Colours can either welcome or alienate. Ultimately, you want your lounge to be a room where family and friends gather and feel they can put their feet up. For this I ask you to give a nod to colour psychology, which can have a profound effect on room mood – otherwise known as vibrational energy. For example, if walls are painted white this can throw out the

impression that you're a detached person who would rather be on their own! But start introducing bolder colours and you begin to look like a girl who likes other people's company. Warm and inviting colours such as orange are associated with love and happiness, or yellow has the habit of lighting up the whole room like it's drenched in sunlight. Conversely, dull shades are linked to a downbeat attitude. You don't even have to paint the whole room – just colour-washing one wall can really change the energy of the room without getting into a huge decorating project.

Hang a mirror

Not only great for checking your lipstick, mirrors work well in a small space, as they are clever room expanders. Just make sure you hang a mirror so that it reflects back something pleasing to the eye. Check out unusual mirrors, too. Venetian ones make the room look elegant, for example, or personally, I like to pick up mirrors in junk shops where the glass is slightly speckled. You could even use mirrors as a design feature. Small mirrors in different shapes look cool when clustered and hung together on one wall.

Hang a chandelier

A chandelier is like hanging beautiful jewels from the ceiling and adds a touch of elegance to the whole room.

Showcase who you are

I find it very suspicious when I go into someone's living room for the first time and I can't tell who they are. By this I mean they have no personality on display. I love the cosy and secure feeling of well-read books, favourite records and piles of CDs in the room as well as bits of artefacts that have been collected and kept for whatever reason. It gives the room a lived-in look and brings stories into the room.

> ### LIFE-LONG TIP
> ★ Treat yourself to freshly bought flowers every week. Not only do they look pretty but they also infuse the room with a natural scent. It's so much nicer than artificial room sprays.

A life lesson in throwing an (unforgettable) house party

You've got your happy home, so why not throw an all-out shindig? Throwing an awesome party should be an event a girl does at least once a year, be it a classy cocktail party or a move-all-the-furniture dance party. You don't even need an excuse to host one. Just do it!

Be spontaneous

Some of the best parties I've been to are the ones that haven't been planned for months. Everybody (especially the hostess) is always a lot more relaxed and loose. Think about it: planning a professional party is much like a wedding. You need to draw up a guest list way in advance. Chances are word gets round that you're throwing a bash and other people within your social outer radar are put out because they haven't been invited. This causes the hostess stress where she then needs to compile another list – this time of excuses. You feel under pressure to make it an out-of-this-world party. People think if you've been planning for months, then it will be a party to rival one Elton John would throw, when all you want is a great little house party with some wicked cocktails, music and funky friends.

My advice is to throw a party when nobody is expecting it (it's not your birthday/Christmas/Easter), and tell friends a week before by word of mouth. This makes the event unexpected and therefore delivers an out-of-the-blue frisson of excitement. You then want to throw a party your guests will remember, not necessarily be impressed by. Your role is to think of yourself as the not-very-perfect hostess where you couldn't give two hoots about whether the glasses match or the canapés colour-coordinate; your skills are in inviting the right mix of people and whipping up a room that's filled with a buzz of energy and sparkling conversation.

People, drink and food

These are the three main factors that make a party spin. First off decide how many people you want to invite – this will be dictated by the size of your room. Don't invite too many as an evening spent like a squashed sardine is no fun. And don't invite too few as it's embarrassing when the room is half-empty – it looks like you don't have enough friends. Start by jotting down a list of definites: all of your friends who get along together and who you can rely on to see the night out without crying/sulking/being sick. Now think about inviting the people you want to get to know that little bit better. Maybe that good-looking guy that's just joined your section at work. This way it doesn't look like you're desperately trying to chat him up, but simply being friendly and inviting him to your do.

Unless you're up for dishing out boxing gloves and acting as a referee, don't invite people who have 'issues' with each other.

For drinks, don't make it overly complicated for yourself. Stock up on beer, (decent) wine and a couple of cocktails you can premix in jugs, such as sangria and margaritas. Don't forget to buy non-alcoholic drinks – it encourages people to pace themselves. So get plenty of fruit juices, water, lemonade and Coke. Add fresh fruit to your shopping list, too, and slice limes, lemons and oranges in advance. If it's summer, you might even want to set up an outdoor bar in the garden so that it frees up the kitchen for food. Stock up on ice, too: nobody likes warm drinks, it reminds them too much of their student years.

As for food, the secret here is to buy lots (it looks like you've bothered) but keep it simple. Pizzas, dips, crisps, cheese,crusty bread, olives and tapas-style dishes all go down well. Don't serve gooey, drippy sauces near the sofa or an expensive rug!

Make the atmosphere funky

As a partygoer there's nothing worse than entering a room that looks as if the last thing it's expecting is a party. The television blaring, the lights are bright and there's no music on. Prepare the room before the onslaught of guests. Unplug the TV, dim the lights – you can either burn candles or replace bulbs with coloured low-wattage bulbs – and consider your music. A great mix of guests can be dampened down with the wrong music. While guests are arriving, start out with laid-back tracks (but not depressing), as this gives people the chance to mellow and chat without shouting into each other's ears. Then, as the evening hots up, so should the music. Get the party really swinging with loud, danceable tracks that have mass appeal which guarantees hips to sway and inhibitions to fall away. Set up a get-to-know-you-better corner too: an area filled with large cushions where people can cosy up rather than dance.

LIFE-LONG TIP

Give your neighbours the nod that you're preparing to party when you send out your invites. This then gives them the chance to go out themselves. If your party goes on until the early hours, pop next door the next morning (not hungover) and give them a bottle of wine.

A life lesson in decluttering

There are many reasons why we turn into clutterbugs. It could simply be because you can't be bothered to throw stuff away, or for more sentimental reasons such as clinging to the past. Whatever your own personal reasons, clutter fugs up your brain. You can't think when your home/desk/life has been taken over by mounds of clutter. Here are ways of getting rid of your excesses.

Are you a clutterbug?

When you open your wardrobe, sit down at your desk, or cast an eye around your home do you feel refreshed and full of get-up-and-go? Or does the sight of squeezed-in clothes (90 per cent of which you don't wear), piles of papers and a messy house make you feel drained of all energy? If you can resonate with the latter then you're a fully signed-up member of the clutterbug club. Clutter is defined as things you no longer use, love or want. It's items that you wore five years ago and fashion dictates you will never wear again, it's empty perfume bottles still on your dressing table, it's piles of old magazines that just keep getting taller and it's an exercise bike in the corner of the room that continues to collect dust. All these things are clutter that create a 'visual noise' in your life and pull your energy levels down. It's time to get rid of them.

Start small and get big

The thought of decluttering can literally be overwhelming, so the idea is to start small – say with your underwear drawer, for example. How many grey pants and washed-out bras are you holding on to? Find them and bin them. It's the same with socks – sort out the odd pairs and find their partners, and throw away any that are left. Chuck out ones with holes. How good does it feel? Believe me, decluttering is better than a workout, it gets the adrenaline going where you just want to do more!

You can then move on to your wardrobe, passing on items that don't fit, are beyond repair, unflattering or should be handed over to the style police. Once you've built up the momentum and felt the thrill, let your decluttering skills go random. Clean out your car, tear out the pages you want to keep from magazines and then recycle, address kitchen clutter (check out all those out-of-date tins) and address your medicine cabinet. Even turn your attention to your computer and delete cyber clutter such as emails and round robins. Always keep the mantra 'out with the old, in with the new' ticking over in your mind and you will begin to create sane living and working space.

How to get over the guilt

Don't be fooled that decluttering is easy if you're not used to it. It can actually be very hard. Tears can fall if sentimental items are binned in a moment of haste. Take your time when decluttering and be selective when dealing with items that bring back memories. By all means keep the special stuff, but store it in a box and put it out of the way. The same with presents; why is it that you're still hanging on to wedding presents (from five years ago) that you dislike? It feels ungrateful to throw away presents, but if you don't like or use them, what's the point? Give them away to a charity shop and dump the guilt. If you're really not sure whether to declutter something or not, set yourself a deadline. If you haven't used or thought about it in three months, then get rid of it.

How do you feel?

I know for a fact that when I'm lying in bed knowing my wardrobe is in control and I have no greying knickers in my drawers I feel cleansed. Crazy, I know, but that's the power decluttering has – it makes you feel revitalised and at peace. It allows you to breathe. Apart from the psychological bonuses there are practical ones, too. Your home will look bigger (piles and junk close in a room), you can actually find your keys, and when you go shopping you can clearly visualise what's in your wardrobe and know what you need.

CHAPTER 4
Friends, Fallouts and Family

A life lesson in handling friends' flashpoints

You know how it is: when your girlfriends experience a major life shake-up so does your relationship. Just like a marriage, friendships can come under great strain when faced with change, and if you don't want to lose them you need to re-evaluate your friendship and find ways to make it work. Here are three common scenarios that can rock the buddy boat.

She's getting married

Sometimes it can seem a case of 'here comes the bride and there goes the friend' – especially if you're single. When you were both single it was fun. You could compare horror stories, double date and laugh out loud when other not-so-close friends got married in hideous meringue dresses. But no more. The talk has become all about The Wedding, all about The Dress and all about The Man. At this point try not to scream when she brings round yet another bridal magazine; instead be excited for her. After all it is her Big Day and you will be a part of it – especially if you're a bridesmaid. The one time you can really bond like never before during this emotive and stressful time in both your lives is by booking a spa trip for just the two of you and recapturing some of the girlie magic you used to have before wedding plans took over. While away, tell her you value her friendship and hope she will still include you in her family life. If she's a good friend, she will be appalled that you even thought she would throw you away like her bouquet.

She's had a baby

You've thrown her a baby shower, shopped in numerous baby stores and reassured her that her waist will return. But since her bouncing baby has been born you haven't been able to connect with her. Her mind seems to be constantly on the baby and she's out the loop on all the gossip. Be patient. Having a baby is a huge lifestyle change; you need to give her the breathing space to get to grips with being a new mother. It's like learning a whole new job in double-quick time or surviving a hurricane! Be as supportive as you can, even if it's popping round and sitting with the baby for a couple of hours so that she can lay her head down. Believe me, that's the best thing a friend can do and she will love you forever. Once she's out of her baby daze (give it at least six months) then she will want your friendship more than ever. The last things she will want to talk about on her girlie night will be nappies, poo and colic.

She's bagged a fabulous new job

If shoulder pads were still in fashion, she'd be wearing them. From having a joint moan about office politics, back-stabbing colleagues and bosses from hell, your friend has now been promoted and is acting like she's running the country. All her corporate talk about allowing yourself 'blue-sky moments' and 'pushing the envelope' are really beginning to get on your nerves. The closest friendships are usually between people who are on a level pegging, but if one of you moves up the ladder it can become a relationship that's imbalanced, and factors such as principles, money and how you spend your spare time can all have an effect. If her friendship is important to you, speak up and tell her you're really pleased she's got promoted, but to kill the Mrs Thatcher routine and try to focus your conversation away from work.

LIFE-LONG TIP

★ Always make time to fit in a friend. Our desire for girlie chats and fun is biological: when stressed out, our bodies produce oxytocin, a hormone that is associated with our need for intimate connection.

A life lesson in match-making your girlfriends

Every well-meaning girl would like to think she was responsible for at least one happy ending in the name of love. But being a matchmaker is no easy feat – as it can backfire in spectacular style. Think you might have found Mr Wonderful for your friend? Well, here are some things to consider.

Don't force a round peg into a square hole

A matchmaker is said to be a person fond of scheming to bring marriages about. Now, I don't really like the word 'scheming', so let's change it to 'helping', and remember the word 'marriage': that means two people who love each other so much they want to be joined at the hip. The first step in playing cupid is asking yourself whether your friend is dating ready (if she's just come out of relationship she may not be looking for romance just now), and why the guy you have in mind for her would be an ideal date? Draw up a mental checklist: do they have the same outlook? Similar tastes in music? There's little point in the hope of flinging two people together when she's looking to travel the world and he's looking for a dreamscape of marriage, two kids and a family car. Also consider their political backgrounds, religion and financial set-ups. They don't need to be two peas in a pod, but it helps if they have some things in common to make this gig work!

Virtual-date them

Before you throw them together, casually mention their names in conversations with each of them. This way you don't automatically create a high-pressure situation that most (sensible) people would shy away from. Don't make it too obvious that you're acting as a fully fledged matchmaker (you can end up looking like a meddling busybody), just gently introduce them into the general banter and build them up in terms of what they look like, their personality and profession. Get the impression over that if they meet it could change the direction of their lives.

Make the meeting casual (not obvious)

You want both parties to feel relaxed, so weave them into a group. A drinks evening round at your place or at the local bar for six or eight people is a fun way to introduce them and allow them to get to know each other better without too much strain or anxiety. Don't tell your other friends that you have your matchmaker hat on either. There's nothing worse for the destined-to-be couple to be constantly monitored throughout the evening with all-knowing grins, nudging and exaggerated winks! This way they can eye each other up from a slight distance. Find a little nugget of information about one of them that will interest the other and throw it into the conversation. With luck, this will get the ball rolling. Then leave them well alone. Remember: you're taking on the role as a matchmaker, not a chaperone!

Don't act as a go-between

Once you've set up the meet-and-greet, step back and let fate take its course. Don't fall into the trap of becoming a go-between for them. If they are fishing for details or compliments encourage them to speak to each other – not you.

Don't feel a failure if it flops

If your matchmaking skills are outwardly rejected and they had less chemistry than a failed science experiment, don't take it personally. Reassure yourself your girlfriend is not rejecting you. In fact, use it to your advantage: find out what she didn't like about him and then use this information to find her a more suitable match. If she ends up resenting you for thinking she would like a guy with an over-inflated ego and not much else, you can comfort yourself that you were only trying to help. You should also know that perhaps you should give up on your matchmaking skills and concentrate on your own love life!

LIFE-LONG TIP

★ Don't exclude your friends from family gatherings because you think you can't matchmake them. A case in point: a friend of mine invited her single girlfriend to her little boy's third birthday party. She ended up swapping telephone numbers with Mr Polkadot, the children's party entertainer. They have been dating ever since.

A life lesson in learning to like his friends

Love your boyfriend but can't stand his friends? It's a common problem and one that needs to be sorted. It puts your guy in an awkward position as well as putting a potential strain on your relationship. Here's how to handle the boys.

Beers, burps and buddies

Like your girlfriends, his mates are very important to him. But unlike your girlfriends their idea of fun is testosterone driven: plenty of beer, plenty of burps and talk that either bores you to death (motor racing/football/horror movies) or talk you'd rather not be a part of (girls and sex), and when it's all done in the comfort of your own lounge it can be difficult to handle. The first rule, however tempting, is not to wage a verbal war against them all to your boyfriend – he will only get defensive about them and be alienated by you. You need to play it cool. One way to deal with the situation is to make arrangements to go out yourself when he invites them over for a night, but gently emphasise the fact that you'd like them to be gone when you get back. Another way to handle the whole situation without looking like you're distancing yourself too much is to go out and come back just in time to share a drink with them. This way you seem charming and sociable before you chuck them out!

Don't make him choose

If you really don't get on with his mates the worse thing you can do is give him an ultimatum: me or them. You'd be gutted if he chose them! I can assure you friendships between guys last and are pretty solid. One of the reasons is because their friendships are not as emotive as girlfriends' relationships and therefore they don't tend to have big fallings out. And the more you begin to see his friends vs you as a love test, the worse the situation will become between you two.

You could be seen as the enemy

One reason why you don't feel a big friendly vibe between yourself and his mates is because they may see you as The Enemy – the one person that threatens to break up their cosy little we're-all-boys-together group. In a way it's flattering to

you: your boy is obviously so in love with you he's caused his mates to break out in a sweat and worry about commitment/marriage/babies and all that other 'girlie' stuff. Furthermore, when one of their group breaks free and starts to cosy on down, it forces them to face up to their own lives. Are they really a sad loser who can't hold down a girlfriend? Ultimately all their insecurities and worries are directed towards you. Don't take it too personally when they start to take the rise out of you and your relationship – remind yourself they're probably slightly envious.

Find something you like about them

Be Zen-like about the situation and encourage good karma by talking to them about their favourite subject: them! All guys love talking about themselves, so really work this to your advantage by asking them what they like, what football team they support, their family … the list is endless (stay with me here, there is a reason for it) and they will be like putty in your manicured hands. Why not even push the boat out and suggest your boyfriend invites them round for a poker night? You aren't swallowing your pride, you're building bridges, which will have your boyfriend loving you even more.

LIFE-LONG TIP

★ *Play matchmaker (see page 79 for tips) and introduce some of your girlfriends to his mates. You never know, there might be fireworks and it will make socialising with them a whole lot easier.*

A life lesson in surviving a (family) Christmas

Ho, ho, ho! It's Christmas and a time when families gather together in the name of peace, goodwill and opening presents. Yeah, right! It can also be a time of arguments, stress and asking, 'Have you got the receipt,' when you open yet another dodgy sweater from Aunt Betty. Here are tips on finding some family festive cheer.

Be cheerful, it's Christmas!

When it comes to celebrating with your friends Christmas is great. It's a continual round of parties, cocktails and kissing under the mistletoe. But when it comes to spending the day at your parents – along with a pick 'n' mix selection of relatives you have nothing in common with and haven't seen since, well, last year – all the festive fun can evaporate faster than air from a pierced balloon. Family get-togethers can be difficult, but there are ways of making them more bearable.

Start by putting on your happy face. After all it's only for one day. Dress up for the occasion – not only will it make you feel better, but you'll receive compliments from Aunty Nelly on how lovely it is to see young girls making an effort these days. Don't bang on about Christmas only being a commercialised exercise that starts in September – it pulls down the mood. Arrive armed with (thoughtful) presents, a box of sweets and crackers. Put on a well-practised smile when they ask if you've got a boyfriend, and if not, why not? And shouldn't you be worried about being left on the shelf? If you mentally prepare yourself for these seasonal questions then you'll be more adept at handling them with grace and humour.

Support your mum

Mums love Christmas, but would love it even more if they got plenty of help with the cooking and washing up. There is usually a line of tradition when it comes to spending Christmas at home: dad does all the nice stuff, like pouring the drinks, roasting the chestnuts and trying out his new slippers for size, while mum is stuck in the kitchen trying to juggle the turkey, roast potatoes and Brussels sprouts. Bring your own pinny and step in and help her. Look at it as an opportunity for some mum-and-daughter bonding as well as escaping the Spanish Inquisition from the relatives.

Turn off the television

It causes arguments. On the one hand you get viewers who want to watch a re-run of their favourite sitcom which you've seen a dozen times before or the ones who demand cinema-like silence when watching a Bond movie – and do lots of tutting when you unwrap a sweet. Instead, take it upon yourself to organise some party games. You either love or hate them, but at Christmas they're essential as they lighten the atmosphere and encourage people to act stupid – or look stupid! Steer clear from games you play with your friends such as truth or dare – you don't want any sordid family secrets rearing their ugly heads. Charades is always a safe bet. Put on some corny Christmas music and get everyone dancing, too.

Act like a (big) kid

No, that's not stamping your feet and having a tantrum, but getting excited about Christmas Day (it's a day off work, for starters) and looking at it through a child's eyes. A child (under the age of five) would never dream of asking for the receipt in the hope of taking a present back, they revel in the comfort of being in the bosom of their family and go gaga over the decorations. If you're lucky enough to be in the company of children on Christmas Day, make the most of it. Play with their toys and take them out on their new bikes and scooters. At least it gets you out the house for a breather!

LIFE-LONG TIP

★ *Don't get stuck in a Christmas rut. What you do one year, you don't have to do the next. Mix it up: invite your parents for Christmas dinner at your place along with some friends. It breaks from tradition and puts a different spin on the day.*

A life lesson in getting on with your mother-in-law

Mothers-in-law (even if you're not married they can be a powerful force in your coupled-up life) have been the brunt of jokes since the beginning of time, but you can either decide to have her on your side or risk causing a rift between your boyfriend and yourself. Here's how to stop his mum turning into your monster-in-law with some coping strategies.

One of the family

Your own mum can be eye-rollingly trying at the best of times, then you meet a great guy and you acquire a mother-in-law. The arrival of a mother-in-law can be difficult, as it sets up a human triangle that can turn into one-upwomanship and, ultimately, rivalry. But like his mates, your man's mother is a very important part of his life and the last thing he wants is for the two women he thinks most of baring their teeth at each other. It causes distance and friction. Hopefully, your mother-in-law will embrace you into the family, if she doesn't, then you have to be grown-up about it and give off a welcoming attitude yourself. Reach out to her and be respectful – even if she says something bitchy and then smiles! Remember: if you're serious about your guy then it's in your best interests to take the high road and realise that you are building a solid base for a happy relationship.

Make a good first impression

This advice was passed on to me by a friend who has managed to clock up quite a few long-term relationships, so therefore has had her fair share of mothers-in-law in and out of marriage. Her first nugget of advice upon first meeting a mother-in-law is always to dress up. 'What you wear makes a big impression,' she says, 'so although it may sound twee to turn up in a pretty skirt and top, it reassures her that her beloved son isn't nestling with a lap dancer.' Next, unless she's struggling to make conversation over the scones, let her take the lead. 'The trick is to let her do all the talking, which you then react to in a positive way. Look interested, nod your head and make encouraging comments.' A small gift always works well – even if it's a bunch of flowers. Pass it over with the words, 'I've heard so much about you,' along with a winning smile.

Becoming part of the family

You know what they say about mothers and their sons, so you have to accept the fact that his mother will probably initially view you as an 'out-law' or at worst an intruder who is going to brainwash her precious son into taking on different habits and attitudes to life. It can be an insecure time for her and therefore she may react to you harshly. Define yourself as a joined-at-the-hip couple early on, encouraging him to talk about plans together such as a holiday, or even getting married, in front of his mum. This will tell her you're serious about each other and you're going to be around for the long term.

Make her a friend

It's great if you can really bond with his mum. It makes family life so much better all round. Try to establish your own relationship with your mum-in-law beyond your husband/boyfriend. Why not take her out to lunch? It can be fun listening to childhood stories about your other half, but don't use her as an informer on your guy's past girlfriends. It will only get back to him and cause resentment and arguments. Ultimately you both love the same man, so that should be enough of a common bond!

LIFE-LONG TIP

★ Be a good daughter-in-law by showing an interest in her family (apart from her son), and be tolerant. Just as your own mum has her annoying little ways, so will your mother-in-law. You just have to accept her for who she is.

CHAPTER 5
Flirting, Fellas and Foreplay

A life lesson in skilful flirting

Flirting is a great sport: it swamps your body with feel-good chemicals and can lift your self-esteem sky high. Flirting reasserts your womanly charms and makes you more attractive, not only to the opposite sex but to others around you, too. Here's how to switch yourself on to flirt mode.

Becoming a natural flirt

For some, flirting is a natural technique. I know one girl who naturally flirts with everybody: men/women/children/doormen – and everybody loves her. She comes across as friendly, warm and sexy without alienating anybody. Which just goes to show that flirting isn't just about attracting men (although it's certainly a good way to hook them in), it's about captivation and ultimately getting what you want! For others, flirting can be hard, or at best, awkward. The thing to remember is that flirting is a social skill, with confidence as the underlying skill. You don't even have to be an out and out flirt – all batting eyelashes and flashes of cleavage – you can be a passive flirt and still reap the benefits. People who aren't natural flirts tend to think of the whole act as a form of manipulation, but really it's an act of honesty as you openly display your interest in another person.

Work it girlfriend!

Although I said flirting can be used on anybody – and it can – it's usually an act reserved for the guys. And they love it. Men love being flirted with and wish girls would do it more. Therefore, you have an unrevoked licence to thrill! Start by working on your smile. It needs to be friendly, open and warm. Think of it as your own personal calling card. A grimace just doesn't cut the mustard. Next, understand that flirting is all about fun, so think of playful thoughts as you set your sights on him. Then catch your victim's eye. Eyes are central to sexual attraction, so make brief eye contact, then look away. Staring or glaring is off-putting. Carry on eye flirting coyly with flashes of glances in quick succession for a couple of minutes. This act will automatically reel him in closer to you.

Keeping your body language open and inviting, lean towards him and introduce yourself. Whispering into his ear is a great flirting technique, as it sets up an innocent intimacy. Compliment him. Men aren't used to being complimented and they readily warm to it, as it shows you've really noticed him. Make your compliment genuine, too, such as, 'I really like the way you look in that shirt.' By now he will be melting, so switch on to your sexual energy by subtly touching him. Touching an arm during conversation to emphasise your point is a non-threatening way to flirt with touch.

How to know if you've won him over

There's little point in flirting if the person you have in your sights isn't interested, so it pays to clue up on body language. The following signs mean he is falling for your charms. He'll fiddle with his clothes. You've put him on the back foot and made him slightly nervous, so he needs a displacement activity. Fiddling with his tie/socks/jacket is also said to be an unconscious wish to whip off his clothes! His eyebrows will take on a life of their own. Eyebrow flashing – they go up and down – is a definite sign he's interested. If not sitting down – he will perch on his seat to move closer to you – he will listen to you with hands resting on his hips. He's hoping you will notice his physique and that you will check out his body. These are all thumbs-up signals. If you sense he's not interested, then save face, back away gracefully with the thought that there are plenty of other men to hone your flirting skills with.

LIFE-LONG TIP

⭐ *Don't flirt if you just want to be friendly. It can give out mixed messages and lead you into trouble. It pays to hit your de-flirt button once in a while.*

A life lesson in seduction secrets

It's often assumed that it's the woman who succumbs to seduction in the dating game, but there's no feeling more powerful than becoming a full-on seductress. Your mission? To capture your prey, lead him astray, tempt him into sin and persuade him to abandon his principles. You will be talked about as a goddess for years to come.

Set yourself up as a girl of mystery

Men like the idea of a 'free spirit', that's a woman who doesn't reveal too much about herself and therefore seems interesting and unattainable. Telling him everything about yourself, from the guy you dated way back when to what colour knickers you're wearing and how you always eat fish on a Friday is not seductive. It's boring. A man initially wants a woman he can fantasise about, one he doesn't know the truth about. This is where seduction can be fun. Start spreading little rumours about yourself: suggest you may be seeing someone, but it's not that serious as it's very complicated. Guys like nothing more than a challenge and if you're half-hearted about the truth it keeps him alert, insecure and very interested. Just the way you like it!

Act like a seductress

This doesn't mean sashaying around like a busty wench wearing a corset, but all sexperts agree that flashing some flesh appeals to a man's primeval sense. So show some skin. The collarbone and the dip of the neck are powerful erogenous zones and can attract him more quickly than a crude showing of an overly exposed thigh or a large expanse of cleavage. Most men are put off by women who look like they try too hard to be sexy. Great posture (seductresses never hunch) and a slight hip sway to your walk always arouses interest, as does a seductive tone of voice. For girls, this is slow and breathy (think of Marilyn when she sang 'Happy Birthday Mr President'), and keep your body language subtly open at all times. That's no crossing of the arms, and when you sit be sure to cross your legs and lean back into your chair. If you lean forward you look way too interested in him. Keep him on his toes.

Be unavailable – some of the time

Seduction shouldn't just be a one-night manoeuvre, it should ideally carry on for weeks. Why not draw out the excitement of wanting and pursuing someone for a little bit longer? He will appreciate it as much as you enjoy it. A competent seductress will never make herself readily available 24/7 during this time. Now and again she should pull back and even ignore him. This will not only leave him frustrated but also give him space and time to fantasise about you even more. Likewise, when talking to him, don't play the role of a nodding dog and agree with everything he has to say. You have a mind of your own – so use it. Men like confident women who air their views, as it will make conversations lively. Play it cool and you will leave him feeling even hotter for you.

Now surrender

Once you've decided that your role as a first-class seductress has been successful (the clue being his tongue is now hanging out like a panting dog, and his pupils well and truly dilated) and you want to take your relationship to the next level, start to make yourself a little vulnerable to his advances. Surrendering might sound like you're throwing in the towel, but if he has red blood running through his veins, he will by now have taken on the role of pursuer where the 'hunter' in him will have begun to track down his 'prey'. He will

appreciate it if you start to let him exhibit his repertoire of seduction skills, otherwise he will start to feel emasculated and move on. Men like a touch of vulnerability in a girl, so humour him and start to act like a damsel, if not in distress, then at least with the willingness to be undressed by him! With all this role playing, there should now be fireworks behind closed doors.

> ### LIFE-LONG TIP
> ★ Hold back from wearing fragrance when in seductress mode. Scent masks the chemicals you produce naturally, called pheromones, which can't be detected consciously, but send men wild.

A life lesson in knowing he's the one

If you can't keep your hands off each other then you're clearly in lust, but what about love? Sometimes it's hard to distinguish between love and lust when in the throes of passion, so how do you know if you've met The One before you decide to move the relationship on? Obviously there are no love guarantees in life, but here's a checklist that he could be your soulmate.

You can be you

Relationship experts believe couples that go on to live together, make cute babies and live happily are the ones that have a natural chemistry from the beginning. You can actually feel it. You don't have to force, push or tug the relationship into shape to fit around either of you – both of you can just be yourself. This in itself is refreshing, as many of us adopt a different persona when first meeting someone we're interested in purely in the hope of impressing them. But it can be hard to keep up this façade (showing your sweetest side all the time can be exhausting) and that's when the relationship can start to crumble. When you have a natural ease in the relationship not only can you feel it but others can see it, too.

You really trust him

Trust is key to an enduring relationship. With no trust it just can't grow. Trust doesn't just mean the fear of him being unfaithful, it means putting a trust in him that he wants the same out of the relationship as you. It also means being able to have fights without the thought of the whole relationship ending. Arguments can actually be healthy for a relationship, as it keeps communication open and you can both voice (or shout) your differences. You know you've got a strong bond when you have the confidence in your relationship that means you can kiss, make-up, sort out why your antlers locked and move on – not out – after the row.

He's your soulmate

Not only do you share common ground but you also know he's always looking out for you. You have this constant sense of security (even when he's not around) and when you talk to him, far from being white noise, he actually listens to you. He may not always give the advice you want to hear – in fact, in true man style he will come up with solutions rather than platitudes – but ultimately you know your interests are his interests, and vice versa. The One will also support you professionally and personally, and not try to compete with you. He pampers you, too. He demonstrates in small ways that you are his one whether it be cooking you a meal, massaging your feet or sorting out your taxes!

He gets the thumbs up from family and friends

If friends and family think he's Mr Wonderful, too, then this counts for a lot. There's nothing more draining in a relationship than if nobody likes him – and there's usually a reason. It can be hard work for you to be constantly PRing him, and the chances are you will end up alienating yourself from your friends and family, and resent him for it. How can he be The One if you have nobody to invite to the wedding?

You just can't hide it

He brings out the best in you (and you him), where you both can't hide your adoration for each other. Your eyes light up when his name is mentioned and you are extremely happy. In fact you glow. The great thing is that once you've met The One you don't feel needy and clingy, as there's nothing to make you feel insecure. It's a relationship that makes you feel free, rather than stifled.

> **LIFE-LONG TIP**
>
> ★ We should only be prepared to change one mind, and that should be our own. If you have to work hard to change his mind on decisions that are central to your life together, then he's not The One.

A life lesson in moving in with him

Congratulations, it's an exciting time; but moving from honeymooning together at the weekends to living together 24/7 can throw up some unexpected challenges beyond 'where the heck am I going to put his revolting seventies-style coffee table?' Here are some things to consider if you want to make it a fairytale ending.

Are you both doing it for the right reasons?

It needs to be said: are you moving in together only because you're fed up with sharing a bathroom with two other flat-mates, or because he needs somewhere to sleep because his landlord has turfed him out? Never underestimate the change in dynamics when you move in together. It's hard to see him as a knight on a white charger when you're picking up his underpants, so it's important you don't feel fast-tracked into cohabiting coupledom, but instead are moving in together for all the right reasons: because you want to – simple as that.

Make it a step forward in your relationship – not a step back

Moving in together is one very big step and you may feel

tempted to give up everything to give it your all. But don't. A common trap to fall into is to give up on your identity – a clue is starting to talk as the royal 'we' along with resigning your power in the relationship. It's important to remember that your guy has fallen for you and everything that entails – even your annoying little habits – so don't feel tempted to give up friends/family/your views just so that you can devote all your time to being what you think is the 'perfect woman'. You're perfect as you are!

Talk, talk and talk (did I say talk?)

First up: talk about what you both want out of the relationship long term. If you're thinking of him as a right-for-now guy and he's thinking of you as his future wife, then things might get a bit tricky in the long run. Think about his differences, too, and whether you can live with them. His penchant for untidiness might be OK round at his flat, but what about when you're living with him? What about his friends? Will the Friday poker night still be an ongoing arrangement round at his – now yours and his? And what about smoking and drinking? A good time in a bar is one thing, but an ashtray full of cigarette butts as a full-time feature in your home might be the one thing that doesn't rock your boat. All of these things need to be thought about and talked out before they cause friction between you.

His place or yours?

If either of you are moving into the other's space then make a pact that you will start thinking about your living space from a new perspective. Neither of you want to feel like a tenant. Don't start by claiming you're going to trash his beloved tatty sofa (wait a few weeks at least), but do make small but compromising steps such as changing the decor – the chances are he would have painted it all grey and you pink, so go for something you can both live with – and swap the furniture around, adding new pieces and fitting in the old along the way. This way neither of you should feel like you're moving into occupied territory.

Sort out the money rules

Your financial priorities, spending and saving habits along with your short- and long-term goals involving money should all be up for having an Oprah moment. All small details should be on the table for discussion; for example, when deciding how much each person can afford on rent and bills you will both need to open up on how much you earn and your liabilities. Don't think that sharing space is just a fast way to pay off your credit card debts. Don't initially apply for a joint credit card (one bad move by your partner could screw up your credit rating) or combine your bank accounts either. However, you might want to think about opening a joint account to which you both contribute enough money to cover all living expenses. Just make sure you both keep separate accounts for all your little luxuries such as shoes and CDs respectively. Trust me, this leads to fewer arguments!

LIFE-LONG TIP

★ If you both own homes and you're thinking of moving in with him, rent out your place for a while rather than selling it. Be smart, too. If you rent space, make sure both your names land on the rent book. It's a smart girl's back up just in case the rose-tinted glasses fall off!

A life lesson in great fore (and after) play

There's little doubt that foreplay is your sexual starter to working up to a much anticipated main course – and you just can't underestimate it for keeping the sizzle going in your relationship. But don't expect your guy to put in all that effort – girls are just as capable of giving fantastic foreplay. Your man doesn't have only one erogenous zone (believe it or not) – he has many. Here's how to assert yourself as a sexual goddess.

Start outside the bedroom

Foreplay doesn't have to happen in between the sheets, in fact pre-passion foreplay can happen hours before you even get into the bedroom – it's all about having an up-front attitude. If you're feeling frisky, why not send him an email or text saying how hot you're feeling for him and that you can't wait until you see him tonight? If you begin foreplay in the morning and carry it through until the afternoon (send another little sexy text after lunch, signed off Miss Naked) and I'll guarantee it won't be his spreadsheets that will be on his mind all day. Another nice little teaser is to post him a sexy fetish Polaroid of yourself (nothing on except shoes), making sure he gets it the morning before the evening you see him.

Just make sure you get them back if you ever split up! Delayed passion builds emotional excitement so be prepared for fireworks later.

Touch, taste and tease

Put all of his senses on high alert. Dress in sensual begging-to-be-touched fabrics such as silk or satin, invite him over for dinner and greet him with a deep, slow kiss. Let his hands wander over your body. He will love the feel of the fabric under his fingertips along with the way it clings, moulds and moves with your body. If you're feeling really racy leave your knickers off. Continue to build on the atmosphere. Cook a delicious-smelling meal (scientists have found that vanilla acts as a potent arouser) and play sensual music. Old soul classics such as Marvin Gaye never fail to hit the spot. Read him a couple of passages from a highly erotic book – it will probably be the last thing he's expecting. Once you've developed all of his senses to breaking point lead him up to the bedroom to finish the final chapter!

Linger and touch

It's not only women who want their bodies to be appreciated, guys do, too. If you've been together for a while, sex may have become a case of whipping your clothes off, slipping under the covers and getting on with it. Go back to taking your time and savouring every moment. Peel off his clothes and let your eyes travel and linger over his body. Run your finger down the middle of his chest and stop just before you hit his genitals. Become a hot tease, run your hair over his body and pay particular attention to his other erogenous zones such as the inner thigh, nipples, ear lobes, tummy and neck. Get as close to intercourse as you possibly can without actual penetration. By now he will be aching for you.

Surprise and delight him

The more you surprise your guy, the more aroused he will be. So get creative with the tip of your tongue, wear amazing underwear he has never seen you in before, tell him your fantasies and what you want him to do to you. You could even try blindfolding him and pouring something you love the taste of, such as honey or cream, over his body and licking it off. If you're really comfortable with him, throw off your inhibitions and pleasure yourself in front of him. The more unexpected you are leading up to sex the more explosive it will be.

Keeping the afterglow burning

After all that seducing it can be tempting to pull on your comfy old pyjamas and go to sleep. But afterplay is just as important as what goes on before sex to keep that lovely just-you-and-him feeling going. A post-coital massage always works on keeping that feeling of cosy intimacy, and don't forget to tell him how good it was for you. Bring up specific things he did that made you go weak at the knees – he will be sure to do them again.

> ### LIFE-LONG TIP
> ★ When you're not new to each other, just be sure to keep doing new things to each other in the lead-up to sex. This way both of you will never become complacent with your love-making, as it keeps things fresh.

A life lesson in being a happy-ever-after couple

What are the secrets to making your relationship go the distance? Although there are no guarantees when it comes to love, relationship experts agree that there are certain core values that make some couples more intimate and stronger to handle the everyday stuff that can drive others to crash and burn. So what are they?

Open your ears (and your mouth)

Listen to each other and you can ride almost anything. But first of all you've got to talk! Never expect your partner to mind-read, if you've got something on your mind, say it. Bottling up feelings can lead to frustration and misery, so, as your grandmother would say, 'get it off your chest'. Guys tend to deal in thoughts rather than words, so if you think he's holding in something, ask him, not, 'How are you feeling?' but 'What are you thinking?' He'll open up more when spoken to this way.

Keep laughing

When you meet someone and friends ask, 'What makes him special?' How many times have you said, 'He makes me laugh?'

Well, don't lose the comedy factor as time creeps on. Keeping a sense of humour is vital in a relationship as it creates a safe and supportive surrounding and gives a feeling of shared intimacy. It might be sick-making on the outside, but couples who come up with silly pet names for each other, and insider jokes and phrases that mean something only to them sets up a type of playfulness and is a sign that they are very comfortable with each other.

When the going gets tough, they tough it out

All couples hit rocky patches, even the seemingly loved-up ones. And when the going gets tough, that doesn't mean running off back to your parents or him camping out on a mate's sofa. Your love contract is between you two, so work it out together and come to an agreement without the involvement of others. It's great to be close to your mum and friends, but I've known relationships that have broken down purely because of the intervention of others. Plus, once you start moaning about your other half to friends and family it makes it hard to put him back into a good light with them.

Remember: your friends and family will always take your side, and his friends and family will back him. Keep your fights between the two of you until they are resolved.

Practise relationship fitness

This means doing things together. Once you're past the let's-just-jump-into-bed-together-every-five-minutes stage, then a couple needs to start diversifying and look for other 'hobbies'. Time spent playing together is an investment in the relationship, as it delivers a relaxed intimacy that strengthens the bond between two people. The activity doesn't have to be expensive or extravagant, it could just be joining a gym and working out together, developing a joint interest for art house movies or learning to speak another language. Creating couple time outside the house (and bedroom) helps bring you closer together.

Treat one another like a friend

Have you ever noticed those couples who treat each other with total disrespect? It's not only embarrassing for the onlookers, but it makes you want to stay single forever. Couples that have no respect for each other don't last – and if they do, they're miserable. You wouldn't bark orders at your friends or never say please or thank you, would you? So, why should your boyfriend be treated any differently? For loved-up longevity it's vital that you treat him (and he treats you) with love and respect. If you start treating each other worse than your nemesis then it's a sure-fire sign that the soul has gone out of your relationship.

> ### LIFE-LONG TIP
> ★ *Never stop hugging. No matter how crazy life gets, always make time for hugs. Huggy power changes the whole atmosphere where you reconnect instead of dumping on each other.*

CHAPTER 6
Diets, Desserts and Dinner Parties

A life lesson in the non-diet diet

Once you declare you're on a diet you set yourself up for failure. If it's low calorie (which most of them are) your food intake will be restrictive, probably leaving you feeling woozy, and deprivation will make you obsess about food. Ultimately, diets mess with your metabolism and your mind, and you can find yourself on a roller coaster of emotions along with weight loss and gain. The answer is not to diet but to set up a wellness eating plan for life and you will naturally drop the pounds.

Think about what you can eat, not what you can't

The secret to a healthy diet is concentrating on including foods you can eat, not the ones you can't. The colours you put on your plate can make all the difference. And it's not just greens – although of course they do count! Research shows that yellows, reds, oranges, blues and purples are just as important. Fruit and vegetables such as blueberries, tomatoes, apricots, pumpkins, corn, peppers and grapefruit are teeming with vital substances called carotenoids and flavonoids. These are classed as 'life force' foods, as they're substances that help to mop up free radicals. You don't need a rainbow on your plate at every meal, but make sure you have a good variety. Doing this, you will find the more unhealthy options you once found yourself drawn to will be squeezed out. Once the body becomes optimally nourished it will simply give up its quest for starchy, salty, fatty foods. These hankerings are often the result of nutrient deficiencies or unbalanced blood sugar levels.

Pare down your portions

It takes no Einstein to work out that big portions add up to more calories, which contribute to expanding waistlines. Dieticians are now viewing portion control as the most important aspect of weight management. As a rough guide, limit your grain portions. Pasta should be likened to the size of a balled fist, and your protein, such as meat, to that of a deck of cards and no bigger than your hand. Affirm that you eat to live, not live to eat. Small, frequent meals keep the metabolism running in high gear, which is a key tip on the energy front. Healthy nibblers tend to have a leaner body mass than those who go for three square meals a day. Fill up on foods such as salads, vegetables, fruits and nuts.

Shop and plan ahead

One of the reasons why people fall off the good food wagon is that they let a pressure-packed situation (stress) interfere with their shopping and therefore their eating habits. How many times have you worked late, got home and looked into a bare cupboard, because you haven't had the time to go shopping, and then ordered in a takeaway? Being too busy to make healthy choices is a common pitfall, so the only answer is to prepare for your week in advance. Take a trip to the supermarket at the beginning of the week so that you're never caught without good foods in your fridge or cupboards. You want items that allow you to whip up quick and nutritious meals, such as tuna, lean meats, tomatoes, pulses, eggs and brown rice.

Never deny your cravings

If you want chocolate, have chocolate. When a girl's feeling emotional it's the only thing to reach for. And don't beat yourself up about it. The occasional binge won't land straight on your hips. A comforting thought is that it takes 3,500 excess calories above your daily calorie allowance of 2,000 to put on 450g (1lb) of fat.

LIFE-LONG TIP

★ *Don't skimp on food. Too little calories in your diet puts your body on famine alert. It will store calories as fat and won't release them for much-needed energy.*

A life lesson in eating yourself gorgeous

Food doesn't only satisfy our stomachs, it's actually one of the best natural beauty tonics going. Your body will readily throw out signs and symptoms of the vitamins and minerals it's deficient in. Here are some top-to-toe clues along with the food sources you need to protect and beautify yourself from the inside out.

Rough, bumpy skin

Skin on the face and the body that's rough-to-the-touch – particularly on the tops of the arms – can be a deficiency in essential fatty acids found in fish, linseeds (flaxseeds), nuts and olive oil. Omega-3s have been found to play an important role in maintaining the moisture barrier function of the skin. Try to eat oily fish a couple of times a week and look to boasting your vitamin E intake, too (sources include: avocado, spinach, peanut butter), which is also attributed to keeping the skin healthy.

Dry and gritty eyes

Dry eyes can be caused by tiredness as well as dehydration caused through staring at a computer screen for too long. They can also be indicative of low carotenoid levels, found in foods such as carrots, sweet potato, watermelon, apricots and brightly coloured fruits and vegetables. Vitamin B2 can also cause dry eyes when a deficiency is present. Find it in foods such as brewer's yeast, liver, whole wheat, almonds and mushrooms.

Brittle and split nails

As well as pointing to a possible calcium deficiency, brittle and split nails can indicate low silica levels, which provide the strength and flexibility of the nails. Cheddar cheese, yogurt and eggs are all good suppliers of calcium, and to ensure you get your quota of silica eat a well-rounded diet that includes alfalfa, rice, oats and brown rice.

Stretch marks

Those angry red lines (which later fade to silver) have been linked to a zinc deficiency. Zinc is a nutrient that's necessary for the production of healthy collagen tissue and for the maintenance of a high level of elasticity in the skin. It's also useful for the metabolism of vitamin A, which keeps the skin lovely and supple as well as strong. Zinc levels can go down by 30 per cent during pregnancy so it makes sense to stock up on this nutrient during this time. It is found in pumpkin seeds, beef, nuts and whole grains.

Varicose veins

These 'old granny' veins occur when the valves in the veins carrying blood back up to the heart become lapse or floppy due to the blood pooling from longer periods of standing, excess weight or generally poor circulation. Foods that help are bioflavonoids, which act as anti-inflammatories and help to maintain the integrity of blood vessels and capillaries along with strengthening connective tissue. Find bioflavonoids in darkly coloured berries such as cranberries, bilberries and purple grapes, along with vegetables such as peppers and tomatoes.

Cellulite

This dreaded orange-skin effect that happily settles around the thighs is not only caused by an excess of bad things (all the usual suspects such as coffee, alcohol and cakes), but can also develop because of a weakness in your collagen supplies. When the body is low in vitamin C the elasticity of collagen collapses and the skin can become susceptible to the bane of cellulite. An increased intake of vitamin C will strengthen the connective tissue in the skin by twisting the strands of collagen, thereby making it stronger. Think of it as being like a thick strand of rope. Fresh foods are a good source of vitamin C (for example, tomatoes, oranges and potatoes), and also look to fibre such as brown rice to encourage bowel movement and eliminate toxins – another cause of cellulite.

LIFE-LONG TIP

★ Research indicates that there are a growing number of women reporting thinning hair. This can be caused by low ferritin levels (a protein that stores iron): a gradual depletion can occur in those who suffer from heavy periods or who are vegetarian. Stock up on sardines, canned tuna and fortified cereals.

A life lesson in the best weight-loss secrets

We've already established that diets are pretty dumb. Let's face it, have you ever met somebody who's followed a diet, lost weight and then kept it off for a very long time? I guess not, so the case is closed. Weight-loss winners are usually girls that have very smart and sensible eating tips tucked up their sleeve. Here are 20 no-diet ways to lose weight that have been tried, tested and definitely work.

1. **Eat your sandwiches naked** Ditch the mayo. Mayonnaise adds up to 70 calories for just two small teaspoons. Having a sandwich minus the mayo is an easy way to cut back on fat.

2. **Distribute your fat** Taking up a Pilates or yoga class will help stretch and elongate your muscles, helping you lose inches and making you look slimmer. To keep your motivation up, measure yourself with a tape measure, instead of weighing yourself on the scales.

3. **Do a Bridget** Keep a food diary. You might think you eat healthily, but check out how much chocolate/crisps/fizzy drinks you consume in a week.

4. **Skip pudding** Make the weekdays pudding-free and then indulge at the weekend. Not only will you save calories but also waiting will make them taste even more delicious.

5. **Eat little and often** Bingeing often happens because blood sugar levels are unstable. Keep them steady and minimise cravings by eating small meals or nutritious snacks every three to four hours.

6. **Fish for your supper** Fish is lower in saturated fat than chicken, beef or pork, so substitute fish for meat up to three times a week. A fish supper protects against heart disease, too.

7. **Pile on the veg** Most people think of the meat as the main event of a meal. The side dish is always an afterthought. Swap it around, so that you think of the vegetables first and then work a small amount of protein

around them. This helps to keep the fat content of the meal down.

8. **Declare the kitchen off-limits** Most pounds are added through 'recreational' eating while sitting on the sofa mindlessly munching and watching television. But remember: you are less aware of what you're eating when occupied with something else. Think of last orders as 7.00 p.m. After that your metabolism starts to slow down so that carbohydrates are more likely to be stored as fat.

9. **Eat breakfast** Skip the first meal of the day and you set up an unhealthy eating pattern for the rest of the morning. Overnight your metabolism has slowed down, so eating straight after you wake up will stoke it back up, helping your body to burn energy more efficiently. Eating cereal, which is high in carbohydrates, makes you feel fuller for longer and therefore reduces the temptation of mid-morning cravings. Bring on the muesli!

10. **Change your habits** Making intelligent food swaps can be the key to weight loss as well as a healthier diet. For example, trade your fruit and nut bar (high in fat, loaded with sugar and low in nutrients) for a couple of squares of dark organic chocolate and a few Brazil nuts (same calories, but boast minerals and essential fats, and are low in sugar).

11. **Colour your tea** Green tea is thought to help you burn more calories at a steady rate as it has a significant effect on fat breakdown. Drink three cups a day.

12. **Shrink your crockery** Eat from a small plate (it will look fuller) and drink all drinks other than water from tall glasses instead of wide tumblers. It's reported that when we drink from a large glass we pour out over three-quarters more than we would for a smaller glass.

13. **Be cocktail smart** Instead of a cream-based cocktail develop a taste for non-fat drinks such as a Bloody Mary. There are fewer calories in tomato juice and it's a potent source of lycopene – a super antioxidant.

14. **Eat slowly** This is one of the fastest ways you can lose weight. You will probably eat less, feel fuller quicker and actually savour the food.

15. **Be aware of low fat** Food companies trumpet the fat-free percentage of the total weight, not of the total calories. These foods are not necessarily lower in calories than their full-fat alternatives.

16. **Watch the drizzling** Salads are deemed healthy, but when drizzled in a high-fat dressing like blue cheese or

thousand island they can turn your greens into the fat content of a dessert! Stick to a splash of olive oil and lemon juice.

17. **Drink lots of water** Water aids weight loss as it suppresses the appetite and increases metabolic function. Get guzzling!

18. **Don't always make food the centrepiece** Look for other ways to make an occasion special without involving huge amounts of food. Book a show or take a group of friends bowling. Refuel your passion for life, rather than your stomach!

19. **Eat when you're hungry** Ask yourself, 'Am I really hungry?' when you pop that apple pie into your mouth, 'Or am I stressed or tired?' If you're stressed, exercise or meditate, if you're tired, rest. Oh, another thing, don't eat just to please people. If your mum insists you have another piece of her home-made cake, just say, 'It was lovely, but no thanks.'

20. **Do the teaspoon diet** Eat pudding with a teaspoon. Your sweet satisfaction will be met, but the time it requires means you're less likely to end up eating the whole dessert.

A life lesson in loving (and living with) that extra bit of weight

Most of us think we would be more popular, sexier and happier if we could only drop that extra bit of weight. But apart from fitting into a smaller dress, there's not much you can achieve from that one thought alone. Your attitude makes all the difference when it comes to feeling hot or not. Here's how to deal with those extra pounds so that you can learn to love your extra padding!

Being loved-up equals extra pounds

Being happy and loved-up more often than not adds up to extra curves. Studies reveal that when cupid first strikes, lovesickness makes us drop 1.3kg (3lb). But once you've settled into the groove of contentment and your heartbeat and adrenaline levels drop down to normal, half a stone (3.2kg, 7lb) piles on. All too often our successes and failures are wrapped up in our weight, but surely being wildly happy along with being a little bit curvier is a small price to pay? If you are feeling unhappy about your size, then write down who and what is making you feel that way. If it's skinny friends making you feel overly plump, then shop with a curvier friend. Of if it's communal changing rooms making you feel a figure failure, order online and try clothes on at home. If these small changes make you feel at peace with your body then perhaps you won't want to diet anyway.

Psychic slimming

Often it's not your size that holds you back, but how you think about it. Think about your size in a positive light and you begin to feel better. In other words psychic slimming! Take your cue from burlesque performers who revel in their curves and walk with an exaggerated sexy prowl. I've seen them in action and it drives men wild and makes women feel decidedly jealous – enough to eat another doughnut! Ultimately, be your own fan club and adopt the mindset that you're gorgeous without denying your natural body shape – female bodies are naturally smooth with their curves softened by fat. If you look in the mirror and clock something you're not so keen on, focus on something you do like, such as your boobs or hourglass waist. Adopt a personal mantra for yourself such as, 'Be who you are, not what you think you should be.'

Don't get obsessed by numbers

What is it about numbers – either on the scales or marked on a label – that makes us feel smug or freaks us out? It's just a number! First off, you will never be the same size in all shops, as they each cut for their particular market. Therefore a shop selling trendy, funky clothes will cut skimpier than a shop full of classic cuts, so be prepared to buy a size bigger in the funkier store. It's no big deal – sexiness comes in all sizes, not just one. If it upsets you that much, simply snip out the offending labels. As for the scales – step off them. You don't need them to feel comfortable – you should feel that in your own skin.

Flatter your figure

Don't hide your shape away – flatter it. Start to think of yourself as Hollywood sexy (when they had hips and breasts!). Dress womanly to show off your shape with sculpting pencil skirts and slinky dresses right down to silky underwear. Take note that anything that moves around the body makes you look a lot bigger than you actually are, so keep frills and flounce to a minimum or wear on the slimmest part of your body. Cool hues such as blues, greens, greys, browns and black all give the cherished effect of shrinking you down a size or two with the added bonus of keeping your curves.

LIFE-LONG TIP

⭐ *According to a study released by the Smell & Taste Treatment and Research Foundation in Chicago, men perceive a woman as being up to 5.5kg (12lb) lighter if she wears a spicy floral fragrance. Sniff out perfumes that smell of strong flowers like tuberose, or spices such as cinnamon, clove, juniper or coriander to create an olfactory illusion.*

A life lesson in socialising and staying slim

How boring life would be if we only ever cooked our own low-calorie meals to ensure a nipped-in waist-line. There's nothing nicer than meeting friends or family in a restaurant and having a good slap-up meal. But however nice, too often and too much can see your dress size double. Yes, it's a well-known fact that those who eat out will scoff in one meal a day's suggested calorie intake. Here are some selective guidelines for dining out.

Make mine a tonic

I'm not saying stay teetotal for the whole meal, but having a slimline tonic as an aperitif will save you some precious calories so that you can then drink wine with your meal. Why? Because a large glass of red wine has almost 200 calories – that's more calories than many foods! Also, alcohol drunk on an empty stomach excites and stimulates your appetite along with reducing your self-control. That bowl of peanuts on the bar will be demolished, adding even more pounds.

Use your loaf!

Like alcohol, beware of how much bread you tuck away.

Usually placed on the table alongside your drink, it's so easy to pig out on it before you've even ordered your meal. Bearing in mind that a small roll has around 84 calories and that's without the butter, you'd be best to skip it altogether if your main meal is pasta or includes potatoes or rice.

Order smart

Make a pact with yourself to order only one indulgent course. If you wind up ordering three courses boasting cheese, chips and cream, and you eat out three or four times a week then you're definitely courting bigger hips! Try to pick one course that's a salad (starter) or a fruit (dessert). Requesting your dressing on the side is always a good move, and don't be tempted to sprinkle the salt. Chefs love salt, so be assured they've seasoned it well before it's even got to your table. Salt makes you thirsty, so you order yet another glass of wine.

Play the word game

This is one of the most important lessons you can learn from dining out. Steamed and grilled good; fried and sautéed not so good! Get the picture? Learn to read a menu like a nutritionist and you can easily socialise and stay slim. Other words that are open for ordering are: 'broiled', 'poached', 'cooked in its own juice', 'garden fresh', 'baked' and 'blanched'. Those that should be thought of as last orders (or never ordered!) are: 'crispy', 'crunchy', 'buttery'. Order dishes cooked in wine or fresh stock rather than cream.

Too much choice

One word: 'buffet'. Another two words: 'portion distortion'. Give us too much choice and we eat it. Be warned: our bodies' inbuilt appetite-regulating mechanisms are easily overridden by the sight, taste and smell of food even when we're not hungry. We are ultimately seduced by quantity rather than quality and along the way forget about the calorie content. When faced with a table laden with every sort of food imaginable it's easy to get carried away and pile up your plate. But be picky, go for salads and fish rather than the quiches and pies. Keep your choices restricted and you won't need to succumb to elastic waistbands!

Share

Yes, it's that simple. Halve your portion and you halve the calories. This works well for side dishes such as French fries or potatoes and for puddings. It also works well for pizza. Many are so large they easily feed two, and you can order a side salad each. For puddings, if there are six of you, order three and share.

LIFE-LONG TIP

If you're having a business lunch, order a salad or fish dish rather than a starchy carbohydrate meal such as pasta. The latter will leave you with 'brain drain' where you feel sluggish in the afternoon. A lighter meal will not only be healthier but also leave you feeling more alert.

A life lesson in throwing an easy (peasy) dinner party

The difference between being a girl and being a grown-up girl is that it's now time to start thinking about throwing a dinner party as opposed to a free-for-all house party. A dinner party gives you the chance to invite round your very best friends (no gatecrashers), entertain and cook for them. If the thought makes you fraught with anxiety, here's the best way to play hostess.

Being a hot hostess

There's nothing nicer than flinging open your front door and welcoming your friends into your own home with the intention of giving them great food and a great time. Although food is important, it's the atmosphere that will make a lasting impression, so make sure you spend some time creating it. It will make your food taste even better! It doesn't have to be all-out posh, but it's nice to set the tone. Make it themed, too. If you're serving Chinese food, for example, why not hang a few Chinese lanterns above the table, or if you're really adventurous and cooking a Moroccan supper why not do away with the tables and chairs and encourage everybody to sit on pillows around a low coffee table? Make your friends feel special by sending them a postcard as an invitation – rather than a casual, why-not-pop-round kind of feel. Encourage them to make an effort and dress up, too. Put 'dress to impress' on the card.

Keep the numbers small

If you've got a small place or you're a novice (and nervous) cook, then for heaven's sake keep your gathering small and intimate. There's nothing worse than over-inviting, making a hash of the food – or worse, not having enough – and feeling very stressed at the end of the evening. Have six at the most. This way you can be confident that you can spend time with all of them and can feed them well. You can also be a relaxed hostess that laughs instead of one that grimaces, swears and stomps around because she has too much to do.

Menu planning

If you make a great effort with mood-enhancing candles, playing funky music, dimming the lights and creating an atmosphere all in the hope that people will overlook the food, then you might come unstuck. The clue is in the name: 'dinner party', so people will arrive with empty tummies in the hope of some good home-cooked food. So what are the menu-planning tricks to reduce hostess stress and minimise last-minute panics? For appetisers keep it fuss-free. Serve in the living room before dinner along with cocktails or drinks. Well-presented and delicious canapés (think melted goat's cheese on small pieces of toast, tasty dips with crudités, smoked salmon wheels stuffed with cream cheese) always go down well and can be eaten casually while sitting down. They're also great if you're hosting alone, as you don't have to worry about popping in and out of the kitchen and clearing the table before the next course.

For the main course, plan in advance. Trawl through a cook-book for a recipe that you can prepare the night before, such as moussaka. If you can't prepare it the night before, think of something tasty but simple you can whip together effortlessly. Salmon, for example, only needs to be wrapped in foil and cooked in the oven for about 15 minutes. Serve with new potatoes and fresh peas mixed with fresh mint. Think about flavours, textures and colours that will sit well on a plate so

that you get a collective 'Ooh' from your friends as you proudly put down the plates.

Dessert time

Whereas you can't buy microwave meals for a main course, a supermarket dessert is acceptable, just make it look like your own! If buying cheesecake, for example, put it on a pretty plate, dust lightly with icing sugar, cut up some fresh fruit and place artistically on top. Otherwise, you can make a fruit fool the night before, pour it into six glasses, pop into the fridge and serve. Why make it hard on yourself?

LIFE-LONG TIP

Buy after-dinner truffles to eat with (freshly ground) coffee, and add a nip of Cointreau/Baileys/Malibu to really round the evening off. It sends friends home feeling fuzzy, warm and loved.

CHAPTER 7
Karma, Knockbacks and Know-how

A life lesson in instant karma

What are the secrets to feeling comfortably blissed out and at peace with yourself without signing up to a hippy tribe? Inner peace can be hard to come by, as small stresses are available for the taking every day. The answer is to find mental escapes as well as practical things you can do to release those pressure-cooking feelings. Take on board these frazzle-proof fixers the stressless swear by.

Three-step rhythmic breathing

What's the big deal about breathing? You do it every day without a second thought, so why do wellness gurus always go on about it? Well, there's a good reason. If you're hooked on stress – and most of us are – then our breathing becomes strained, distorted and shallow to the point where your inhalation levels are affected along with your entire system. When a person breathes inefficiently the effect is that they are not exchanging oxygen and carbon dioxide efficiently, which means that your body is not getting what it needs to function well, nor is it fully eliminating waste. Therefore, you are more likely to feel fatigued and angst ridden.

In relaxation and wellness circles, more attention is being

spotlighted on Three-step Rhythmic Breathing (3 SRB), which is not a breathing exercise, but is simply the natural rhythmic way of breathing – a skill we were born with and then eventually lose. To establish the correct rhythm of breathing, inhalation should take three seconds and exhalation two seconds. So, start now by consciously counting 1-2-3 while breathing in, and 5-6 while breathing out. Four is not counted. To master it, you must try to complete 12 cycles of breathing in a minute – many of us find we breathe beyond 18 cycles a minute. Take time to study it and you will achieve control over stray thoughts, focus your concentration and lower your blood pressure.

Picture your (ideal) life

We give so little time to thinking about where we're heading and what we actually want from our lives. We are so busy running around meeting crazy deadlines that we rarely take a minute out to calm our minds. Whenever you feel the need to 'regroup' with yourself (usually after a tense day), find half an hour of uninterrupted quiet time – just before bed is good – and create a detailed visualisation in your mind of your ideal life. It may be wishful thinking by any other means, but not getting sidetracked into the realities of your life can really help your mind expand. Picture where you eventually want to live, with whom and what you will be doing. Do you have children? Where do you holiday? The purpose of this role play is to tap into your ideal life wish list – it also helps by throwing up goals or plans that you may have forgotten you had. Afterwards jot down notes. The next day review them and look for things in your thinking list that you can actually start applying, however small, in your real life. Just feeling in control of your thoughts will help you feel a little more chilled.

Be a knit wit

I admit it doesn't sound sexy or show stopping, but knitting is fast becoming the secret of many a stressless grown-up girl, where it's being hailed as the new yoga. Yes really! Knitting is the comfort food of craft and those getting into the stitch – including Hollywood actresses who prefer to drop one, purl one on set – say it burns off anxiety. Apparently its karmic effects come from the repetitive rhythms of needles, wool and hands.

Tune out to tune in

We all like to be up on current affairs, but let's face it: news-readers and newspapers never seem to report good news! If you're feeling tense, then taking on board reports about war, famine, murder and crime will do nothing to make you feel at peace with yourself. People who are stressed will always inter-nalise distressing news, so for one week try to tune out of global issues and see how much calmer you feel. I've tried it and it really works!

LIFE-LONG TIP

★ Buy yourself happy flowers. Behavioural researchers have discovered that pretty blooms trigger happy emotions and heighten feelings of satisfaction. So fill your vases with sunflowers, daisies and lilac.

A life lesson in emotional intelligence

Forget about IQ – who wants to belong to Mensa anyway? Research shows that your EQ (emotional quotient), or to refer to it by its other name, emotional intelligence (EI), gets you further in love 'n' life than solving mind-boggling puzzles. EI is all about how you handle your feelings and those of others. It's about having empathy, but ultimately getting what you want – in a good way! Check out these smart tips on handling your emotions.

Don't lose it, keep it

In a heated situation who hasn't 'lost it' and then instantly regretted it? When put in a situation where you instantly see red (for anger) take a moment to distance yourself from the circumstances. Take a precious breather to focus all your pent-up energy on knowing what you want to get out of this battle of minds and words. This will give you the space to respond constructively rather than emotionally. This might also mean letting go of your ego. If you've lost your temper because someone has criticised you for a suggestion that you've put forward, it's natural to go into a tailspin and become hyper-sensitive and defensive. But far from telling them to 'forget the whole thing', listen to their reasons on why they have decided to reject your idea or thoughts. Remember: once you're seen with a big chip on your shoulder people are more likely to react to you negatively, or may not even include you in things at all. Learning to reason with your emotions lets you consider the other person's point of view rationally. You never know, they could be right! Admitting when you're wrong is a big boost to your emotional intelligence.

Sharpen up your vocabulary

Words can harm or they can warm. Keeping communication honest and direct can help earn you extra brownie points in life. The secret here is knowing what you want to say and saying it so that it comes across as genuine. There's nothing worse than hearing a rent-a-dialogue that sounds unfeeling and shallow. It also means learning to become more fluid in what you say – after all, people aren't mind-readers, so you gotta tell them what you want! So often we express our feelings in just one word or sentence when there's a whole vocabulary that we can use to convey how other people make us feel. Many of us use a very limited word check for emotions: love, hate, fear, for instance. But getting more accurate in naming your feelings will help express how you feel, and it puts you back in control by connecting to others better. So, for example, if a friend blows you out for the third time running, instead of saying, 'Oh, that's fine,' and putting down the phone seething, say something like, 'I'm really upset and disappointed that you keep cancelling me, is there a reason for it?' This way you're telling her how you feel and then giving her the opportunity to explain herself. Those with a high EI don't tend to hold grudges.

Diarise your thoughts

To crank up your EI factor try jotting down how you feel. It might feel self-indulgent, but it works as an insightful source of information. Reading over your thoughts a day, week or even a month later can help you approach things differently. Writing down your feelings works on so many levels. Firstly, it acts as an outlet for angst, which can only be good news for your health (feeling continually pent up causes your heart to beat faster and therefore for you to feel stressed). Secondly, so many of us can find our true 'voice' through our writing.

Handle the difficult with a smile

The key to becoming super-smart on the emotional front is digging out the psychologist in you. This means being emotionally intelligent enough to realise that difficult people are sometimes not driven by a desire to be very annoying, but sometimes it's more a case of a take-notice-of-me mentality. The secret here is being cool. When trying to manage the downright difficult, the skill is to remain measured and controlled. As well as letting your emotional dictionary kick in, give yourself the mental instruction to relax. Lower your shoulders from ear level and smile. Yes, smile, it shows good feeling! When we give ourselves a conscious instruction to relax, it reassures other people's behaviour, too, so they also act in a calm way.

LIFE-LONG TIP

★ Listen to the (emotionally) wise. It's been found that IQ peaks in the later teens and then levels off, but your EI score increases significantly with age, peaking in the late forties or early fifties. There's little doubt that emotional maturity comes with experience – so listen to your elders!

A life lesson in getting over him

He's gone and it hurts. Whether it was your decision or his, whether you were made for each other or not, a split is still heartbreaking. But your world can't stop spinning and you need to mourn and then move on. Here are a few suggestions on doing it.

Throw yourself a pity party

You're entitled to drown your sorrows and wallow, so allow yourself to cry, throw things, scream, stamp your feet and gaze at photos of him – unless you want to actually pin them on a dartboard. Letting it all out is one way you can move on from him and not stay bitter and twisted. Do not isolate yourself during this time, invite your friends round to share your sorrow. Chances are you've probably neglected them of late anyway if you've been going through a rough time pre-break-up, so take yourself off your island and invite them round to spill out your whole sorry story to. They will be full of much-needed platitudes, making you feel secure and loved. Use this grieving time well by talking it out to help you express your emotions. Although a break-up can seem like forever to get over, be comforted that one day you will wake up and he won't be the first thing on your mind.

Don't have a haircut

It's a cardinal rule that you don't want to cut that man right out of your hair. There has been many a tragic hair tale where grown-up girls have marched to their stylist demanding their locks be cut off in search of a new identity. Don't do it. The gamine look – an ultra-short crop – may look great on Audrey Hepburn but will show off a puffed up face from too much crying as well as any chin wobbles! Go for a trim and an injection of colour by all means, but hang on to your locks unless you want to shed more tears. Look for other ways to bolster your self-esteem by booking in for a facial or buying some new make-up or clothes.

Do something that makes you excited!

Get out of your comfort zone. You've probably been in it for so long you've grown mould! It's easy to fall into a comfy rut when you're in a relationship, and it can go something like: work/telly/bed. Now's your chance to shake off the shackles of coupledom (before you meet your next guy) and liberate yourself by doing something out of the ordinary. The possibilities are endless: you could skydive, take up kick boxing or another kind of martial art (great for pent-up aggression), do a home-correspondence course to further your career (now you haven't got to keep him company on the sofa) or even move out of the area. Essentially, any change will make you feel alive again, get your adrenaline going and put a different perspective on things as well as bless you with a sense of accomplishment because you did it all by yourself.

Pretend he has fallen off the planet

You will never get over him if you're constantly dialling or texting him, whether it's to shout at him or to tell him how much you miss him. Pretend he has moved away and he is absolutely, 100 per cent incommunicado! And don't fall into the trap of ex-sex either. This can happen when he's just 'popping' round to pick up the last of his stuff and you're feeling vulnerable. All too quickly you're feverishly kissing and rolling around in the duvet. We all know make-up sex can be fantastic, but break-up sex always leaves you feeling empty afterwards especially when he dresses and leaves. Remove yourself from temptation by being out if you know he's going to call round.

Sweeten yourself up

The break-up diet where you lose weight effortlessly without even trying gives you permission to eat the most mouth-watering, the most exquisite and the most calorific hand-made Belgian chocolates or ice-cream. The science says you can: chocolate boasts a natural amphetamine called phenylethylamine (PEA) also dubbed the 'love drug', which is the same chemical our brains manufacture to raise blood glucose levels and make us feel dizzy in love. When love dies, we suffer from PEA withdrawal.

> **LIFE-LONG TIP**
> ★ *Don't keep his shirt for a sentimental keepsake. Research reveals that we get physically addicted to the pheromones secreted by the person we sleep with. Chuck it out and wash your duvet, pronto.*

A life lesson in handling change

Your life can suddenly change for all sorts of reasons and sometimes there's nothing in your power that can stop the events. It could be anything from being made redundant to your best friend deciding to up sticks and live in another country. Change can bring on many emotions but the first one that usually sets in is the fear of the unexpected. Here's how to embrace uncertainty, helping you not only to survive but also to thrive!

It's fine to feel worried

Adapting to new situations isn't easy, so it's fine to feel angsty about it. In fact it's good to feel anxiety, as the pressure allows you to sit down and work the changes through in your head piece by piece. If you bury your fears without listening to your negative thoughts, you may wind up acting on impulse and doing something that won't benefit you in the long run. For example, a friend of mine was swiftly made redundant, but instead of sitting down and thinking it through, she panicked, applied for the first job that called for her skills and landed up in a position she hated. She confessed that if she had allowed herself time to worry for longer she would have realised that she didn't actually want to be an accountant any more and would have used her redundancy money to retrain as something else. As it is she has taken on more financial responsibility and can't allow herself that sabbatical.

Don't let the thought of change stop you

So often we are mentally paralysed by the thought of our lives changing and so we never lift our head above the parapet. Change can be good – it keeps life fresh and interesting. Re-evaluate your goals often and don't be afraid to change them if necessary. If you're scared of making big changes – moving house, switching career or packing up everything to go travelling – start making small changes frequently. It could be anything from changing your route to work to going out for a drink with different people in your office. You could even enrol for challenging lessons such as a cordon bleu cookery course or salsa dancing. By doing and seeking out different things you will soon realise that change isn't so hard, or so scary, and that there's a whole diverse world out there waiting for you to grab with both hands. The more you live with the unknown, the stronger you'll be.

Grow and learn

When changes happen that rock your world – a sick parent or an impending divorce, for example – the two most common reactions are disbelief and panic. It's normal to think, 'Why is this happening to me?' and then bury your head in the sand like an ostrich or go into deep hibernation. It's never easy to face serious emotional changes head on, but it needs to be done to give you power over your situation. Talk about your fears with close friends and get their perspective. Their support, help and advice will help you cope with the unthinkable. Remain true to yourself and grow and learn from the experiences. A friend of mine was a complete daddy's girl and when her dad died she thought her world had ended. But she unexpectedly got very close to her mother after his death – they were never very close before – and she realised some good had come out of something heartbreaking. Some changes have the habit of making you grow up very quickly indeed, but this can be a good thing as you will continue to learn and grown within yourself.

Don't look back

Accept that change has happened in your life, no matter how hard, and try to stop dwelling on how things used to be. It won't make matters change. Focus on the now, by thinking how you can improve on your situation or ways in which you can cope with it. If it means reading self-help books or talking to professional people, do it. Figure out what's fixable and take your new life forward.

LIFE-LONG TIP

★ When big changes happen it helps to keep some things in your life constant. Change can make you feel overwhelmed, so create stability by keeping those small comforts going, such as daily chats to your best friend, ordering your cappuccino in the morning or watching your favourite TV show once a week.

A life lesson in being your own personal trainer

A personal trainer's job is to motivate bodies to become fit and svelte that would be more than happy to stay sitting on the sofa. Getting into shape can be tough without joined-at-the-hip help, but you can do it solo by energising your fed-up body with a programme that not only gets you moving but challenged, too. Here's how to break some sweat.

Beat body boredom

To keep making those frequent trips to the gym, the secret is keeping your workouts box-fresh. Doing the same thing over and over again until your body feels like it's on a hamster wheel is not a good thing. Up to 80 per cent of people who work out aren't improving their fitness levels at all because they're not surprising their body every time they exercise. If you're having fun with your workout, it makes sense that you're going to stick with it. Lose the fun and you lose the feel-good factor!

One way of keeping it enjoyable is not turning into an exercise purist. Sticking to the same discipline not only becomes tiresome but can also hinder your performance. Muscles have memory: if they're forced to do the same movements they will quickly adapt and quit responding. Shock your body by working it in different ways: instead of running, exercise legs with a combination of walking lunges, reverse lunges and jumping rope. Fuse your exercise options too: mix a cardiovascular-led workout (aerobics or spinning) with a 'softer' option such as Pilates or yoga to work the body holistically. This way you get strength and tone. To make their clients' exercise programmes productive, trainers modify their programmes every six to eight weeks. You should do the same.

Eat yourself fit

A top-notch personal trainer will always advise on nutrition, as it makes a great contribution towards helping you to train efficiently and is vital for recovery between sessions. Aim for plenty of wholesome starchy carbohydrate foods such as wholewheat pasta, wholegrain breads and breakfast cereals. These contain complex carbs that replenish glycogen stores (stored energy) in your muscles and are your main source of fuel. They are also rich in B vitamins that support energy production. Fluid is obviously important, dehydration is associated with a decrease in both physical and mental performance. You should drink about 500ml (18fl oz) just before exercising and then top up your fluid levels with around 100–300ml (3½fl oz–½ pint) every 10 to 15 minutes. The ideal post-workout snack should be rich in carbohydrates and contain a little protein. Home-made milkshake, yogurt, or a chicken or tuna sandwich is ideal.

Interval train

This is a trainer's secret weapon for fast and efficient results. The definition of interval training is repeated bouts of exercise separated by rest intervals – in other words a programme that alternates between periods of fast exercise with periods of slower exercising. The treadmill is ideal for this: run at high intensity levels on a steep incline for several minutes then reduce the level and slow jog or walk for a recovery period two to three times longer. Aim for a total of 30 minutes with bursts of work-that-body-harder hits combined with take-it-easy slow downs. This way you can start getting the heart beating and the calories burning. Even when you've finished your workout your body will still be burning fat.

Keep a positive attitude

Measure your results to keep you motivated. Keep a fitness diary of the small things you notice about yourself that are changing: you have more energy, you're feeling mentally more alert, you have a bigger appetite but craving healthier foods – this is the magic of exercise! Get someone to take a photograph of you in your workout gear once a month and compare the difference. Keeping a positive mental attitude will help keep you training.

LIFE-LONG TIP

★ *Whatever your workout, aim to push your-self to do that little bit more. If swimming, add in more lengths every other week, if jogging increase your distance and improve your time by the end of the month.*

A life lesson in putting an honest spin on your life

Spinning your life in both work and play is really just a case of adopting a new-you attitude, as the key to projecting an air of success is all in your head. Start to think you're fabulous and others will, too! The art to putting your life on spin is learning to leave out the not-so-good bits (who needs to know you've been sacked or dumped?) and play up all of your good bits so that you come across as nothing short of dynamic.

Be your own poster girl

Don't talk about your achievements – or lack of them in life – in a downbeat tone. It will make you sound uninteresting and a number-one loser. If you can't talk about yourself in a positive light, then how can you expect others to be enthusiastic about you? Learn to be your own PR consultant to the point where you sound passionate and upbeat. When going for a job interview, for instance, walk in with your head held high (it shows optimism), sound engaging by keeping your tone of voice light, keen and animated, and identify your strengths, not your weaknesses. Skip over the point where you flunked out of university and talk up the positive experiences and how much you learned through travelling – the people you met, the countries you saw, the languages you dabbled in and ultimately the benefits from these experiences that you'll be able to bring to the job.

Make yourself sound like you're not one to follow the herd: you seek creativity and develop your team-management skills in unique ways. If you're stuck on what your strengths are, ask your girlfriends and family what qualities you have that make you stand out from the rest (except for your late-night party tricks!). Surprise the crowd and you will upstage the competition!

Get over your failures

We all fail from time to time, whether it's in our personal lives or our work lives, the secret is to learn from it and move on.

Do not keep repeating your failures to yourself or others. The more you play them back the harder it is to fast-forward from them. Berating yourself constantly over your failures will leave you feeling frustrated with yourself – after all you can't change past events – and it becomes a huge energy drainer. The secret of a spin doctor is verbally to round off the edges on a sharp angle, so that everything looks a lot smoother. Do it here, by softening the blow of your failures – 'it wasn't the right time for me to take on such a responsible position,' in answer to why you were passed over for promotion – and then start to look to the future.

Look like you're loving life

Even when the chips are down it pays to smile. Nobody loves a whinger/sulker/self-pitier for too long, so develop your sound bites and snappy phrases. 'I want to spend more time with my devoted family,' is always a good one from philandering and sacked politicians, or 'I'm in a good place right now and never happier,' is another one from a celebrity who's been dumped by another (higher profile) celebrity. Even if people aren't wholly convinced by your spin, you are elevating your life from the temporary murkier depths it's landed itself in, and you are spinning the impression that it's just one of life's little hiccups.

LIFE-LONG TIP

★ *Adopt a positive vocabulary. Using words such as: 'fulfilled', as in 'I'm artistically fulfilled' or 'personally fulfilled', always reflects that your life is going well in people's minds. As does, 'I'm feeling wonderful', when asked 'How are you?' rather than just a plain old flat 'fine'.*

CHAPTER 8
Self-love, Self-help and Self-sufficiency

A life lesson in finding a job you love

Hate the job you're in? Got that Monday-morning don't-want-to-go-in feeling? If you literally tick off the days until the weekend and whinge about your job so much that your friends have started to refuse your phone calls, then it's time to rethink your career and apply for a job with (life) prospects.

Have you got I-hate-work-itis?

To confirm that you're well and truly disillusioned with your job – and not just in a bad mood – ask yourself these questions:

1. Do you start feeling depressed from Sunday afternoon with the thought of Monday morning?

2. Do you purposely always stand next to people with colds in the hope of catching one so that you can have time off work?

3. Do you visualise terrible things happening to your boss?

4. When people ask about your job do you reply, 'It pays the bills'?

172

If you answered yes to three or more of these, then it's blatantly obvious you need a career kick up the butt. The first question you must ask yourself and reply honestly is: 'Is the actual work a problem, or is just me?' If you have problems in one job, they will follow you to your next position unless they are solved within yourself. The secret is finding solutions and taking responsibility for your own happiness.

Day dream: part one

A great get-ahead tip is to let your mind work overtime for you. The first step in any job switch is to pinpoint why you're looking for a change. It's important to conclude why you are unhappy in your current job and whether you are trying to move away from something or someone (bitchy colleagues, for example) or whether you're aiming to move towards something bigger for yourself. Career experts reveal that as well as creating a personal vision of where you ultimately see yourself, you also need to specify your goals. A helpful way of establishing this is to ask yourself the following:

1. What is your ideal workday? Include the maximum travelling time you're willing to put in.

2. What salary do you require to live comfortably on?

3. Would you consider being freelance?

4. What is your ideal position? Outline the tasks and responsibility that you're willing to take on.

Don't be intimidated when writing down your wildest career fantasy: the exercise here is to outline what you really want from your working life. Not what you think you can't get.

Day dream: part two

OK, the second part in this exercise is to list your interests. You know the saying 'find something you love and get paid for it'? Well, this is the aim of this task. Over the next week or so, do an All About Me test where you jot down the answers to the following:

1. What are your preferred types of books – crime/popular culture/historic?

2. What kind of magazines do you read?

3. Which section do you always read first in the paper?

4. What were your favourite lessons at school/college/university?

5. What are your interests?

6. What kind of films do you like?

7. What's your ideal way to spend a day?

8. What are your true values?

9. Ideally if you could solve one global problem what would it be?

10. What personal achievement (outside work) have you been most proud of?

These are just for starters; the idea here is to list all your interests. Now you should have a better understanding of what you're looking for (more contact with the public? less pay but shorter hours?), as well as your areas of interest (photography? writing? research?) and your values (the environment? education?). Interests and values can be your pathway to finding yourself a job where you're going to be fulfilled. Why? Because your personal beliefs are at the centre of what makes you tick and motivates you. When you find work that synchronises with your interests and values it will feel like you were born to do this rather than work to pay the bills. In essence: you will have a sense of satisfaction and importance about the work you are doing.

Look down every avenue

I was commissioned to write a career page each month for a magazine where the angle of the feature was to interview women who were successful in their jobs and how they got there. And, wow, what an inspiration they were! Interests and values were at the core of their careers. One woman loved flowers and decided to take a two-day floristry course just in the hope of arranging blooms so that they looked better in a vase. It changed her life. She offered her services free on a Saturday in a flower shop that she had always admired and eventually packed her job up as a hairdresser, compiled a business plan and set up her own business. She now runs her own flower boutique and has never been happier. Another woman enjoyed organising her wedding so much she researched the market for a year and became a professional wedding planner. She now works all summer calming and organising brides-to-be and takes off the whole of October and November to enjoy her profits! Know your interests and your abilities, and the job you love is well within your grasp.

LIFE-LONG TIP

★ *Take your time if you are thinking of a career switch. It pays to do your research and gather new information bit by bit. You may have to stay in the job you hate just to build up financial backup, but if you can pull it off to complete the bigger picture it will be worth it.*

A life lesson in charming everyone

Learn to charm the pants off people and your life will run a whole lot smoother and sweeter! Some girls are born with the gift of charm, where they effortlessly make friends and influence people, but for those who need to polish up their schmoozing skills, then rest assured that it can be done. Once you understand how to charm with the best of them it will become part of your personality.

Be sincere not superficial

There's nothing worse than being introduced to somebody whose eyes are constantly swivelling around to see who else they can move on to. Or if they ask you a question, nod unenthusiastically to your answer with their (swivelling) eyes now glazed. The first step to joining charm school is to be sincere in everything that you do. That means whether it's greeting someone or telling them to get lost! Charm needs to be sincere – so look the person straight in the eyes so that you at least look attentive, and listen to their answers. Responding with a small nod (not a forced up and down nod which can be concluded as OTT) with tiny verbal clues such as, 'That sounds wonderful,' or 'Oh, really, how interesting,' shows you are listening.

Compliment and compare

This does not mean being creepy or phoney. Charm isn't sexually driven or to be dished out every five seconds, it's an art of giving out warmth and sincerity. An easy way to charm somebody (man, woman or child) is to make one small compliment about them – it could be anything from a necklace they're wearing, the colour of their eyes or the way in which they style their hair. If you make people feel good about themselves, it will put them in a good place whereby they will be putty in your hands! But never confuse a well-handed compliment with flattery. Flattery is normally seen to have an ulterior motive; charm is just your way of being. Next, if the person seems hard to win round, draw a gentle comparison between them and yourself. It could be that they live in the same area as you or you admire the same film director. Offer them a piece of common ground between you both and their antennae will tune into you.

Don't brag

Nobody likes a show-off. The most skilful of charmers will always do themselves a slight disservice and highlight funny little anecdotes about themselves that put them in the wings rather than the spotlight. Only the charming will have the inner confidence to be self-deprecating about their personality or appearance. And only the cocksure will talk themselves up. A charmer knows that throwing open their insecurities will make others instantly warm to them, as it has the reverse habit of making people feel more secure in their presence. Although, be careful how you portray yourself. You don't want to be remembered as a loser! Soul baring isn't charming; it can just be awkward and embarrassing.

Be polite to everybody

Good manners are not negotiable. I was with (who I thought) was the most charming woman at dinner one evening and she was utterly rude to the waitress. Needless to say, I never want to dine with her again. Charm is doing everything pleasantly and lightly, whether it's asking for a drink or sending back a dodgy-looking piece of chicken.

Don't be a Miss Goody-Goody

Charm should be an extension of your good self, so don't fall into the trap of making yourself saccharine coated. Don't be a constant nodder, afraid to air your views (a charismatic person is never bland). Some of the best charmers are a little controversial, as it shows spark and wit. When greeting some-body new, stop yourself from grinning like a Cheshire cat. It looks false and unnatural. Offer them a slight smile (one that's obviously just meant for them) along with a gentle handshake to put them at their ease. Don't act as if they are your new best friend. This is annoying and way too chummy. Don't bombard them with a roll-call of platitudes, either – it comes across as desperate. And finally, clock their body language: if they lean in, you've won them over. If they start backing off, move on!

A life lesson in therapy

Twenty years ago to say you were seeing a therapist was like admitting you had surrendered yourself to the men in white coats as an open invitation to throw you into a padded cell. But fast-forward to this tell-it-all culture and therapy is booming – with no stigma attached. In fact, you'd be thought crazy if you found yourself in the throes of an emotional turmoil and didn't seek a talking cure if needed.

Why talk to a therapist (and not your friends)?

People hunt out counsellors and therapists for a huge number of reasons. If you feel you are not functioning as you should be and carry psychological problems, you may benefit from talking to somebody. Therapists don't know you from Adam, know nothing about your background – until you tell them – and therefore don't judge you. Although friends and family can provide an emotional cushion and a listening ear, it's fair to say that they will have a forthright opinion on your problem, as they know you so well. They just can't help offering advice, whether it's right or not! It's also not fully understood that sometimes a professional mind is needed, because when you are experiencing seriously life-changing events it can sometimes lead to depression, phobias and panic attacks, which can easily get out of control. The idea of therapy is to help you come to terms with your situation and see life more positively. There are many types of therapy but generally they fall into three categories: behavioural, psycho-analytical and humanistic therapies. Here's a brief low-down on what to expect on the couch.

Behavioural

Cognitive behavioural therapy (CBT) concentrates on the 'here and now' as opposed to focusing on past issues. One of the beneficial ways in which CBT works is looking at thought patterns to improve your current state of mind. It has been found helpful in areas such as anxiety, depression and social phobias. It's a therapy that is said to make sense of over-whelming problems by breaking them down into smaller, more digestible parts. This in turn makes it easier to see how they fit together and how they affect you. The five parts are: the situation, your thoughts, your emotions, your physical feelings and, finally, your actions. The philosophy behind CBT is that there are helpful and unhelpful ways of reacting to most situations depending on how you deliberate about them.

To help with this theory your therapist may ask you to keep a diary and to jot down your arrangement of thoughts, emotions and actions to identify the way you handle things. Your therapist will then help you work out how to change your unhelpful thoughts into more positive ones.

Psychoanalytical

This therapy focuses on a therapist listening to your experiences and reviving childhood memories, relationships and traumas that may be buried deep within you. It aims to help you understand more about yourself and your relationships. In theory it's based on mental functioning that acknowledges underlying perceptions, thoughts and desires that you may not even be consciously aware of – or may not want to face up to. Developed by Sigmund Freud, this practice encourages you to talk freely and openly to the therapist about thoughts entering your mind. The therapist will interpret these thoughts and make suggestions, taking into consideration previous unconscious memories that you may have had that will help you understand yourself more and gain control of your life. This kind of therapy can be intensive with several sessions needed each week.

Humanistic

This type of counselling became known over 50 years ago and focuses on recognising human capabilities in areas such as creativity, personal growth and choice. Not as well known as the previous two therapies, it's seen as 'artistic' rather than 'scientific' where its core is to help the client approach a stronger and healthier sense of self – which is also called self-actualisation. This therapy tries to be relatively non-directive (so the counsellor will allow you to guide yourself through the episode rather than being led), since the emphasis is on helping you achieve the capacity for making your own choices.

> ### LIFE-LONG TIP
> ★ Always ask for a full profile of your therapist – you don't want to be spilling out your whole life laundry to an unqualified charlatan! For confirmation of their expertise ask for their qualifications along with their insurance and ask to see their registration details with a recognised body.

A life lesson in schmoozing

Networking (or schmoozing) has become a skill in its own right: do it well and your calls will be promptly returned. Do it wrongly and your calls will remain unreturned. Unfortunately, networking doesn't seem to be an option in the world of work, as it's become an absolute must if you want to get ahead. Here are ways to make good contact.

Make networking select (not overly direct)

Personally, I hate the actual idea of networking – it sounds smarmy and false when you purposely introduce yourself to someone with the hope of getting work in the future. But networking at its most basic is modestly classed as 'talking to people' so, far from making it an ulterior motive, I think the best way to go about it is making it into an occasion where you simply put yourself in a position to hear other people's comings and goings. Make yourself endlessly enquiring and inquisitive about people and you will come away with valuable information. Keep the conversation as natural and light as possible and the chances are something will come out of it – if not immediately, then weeks or months later.

I think the worst kind of networking is when somebody

purposely guns for a captain of industry or some kind of work VIP at a cocktail party, for example, with no thought for anybody else. They will push people out of their path, and go out of their way embarrassingly to overly compliment the 'victim' and their achievements before extracting their direct line. Networking ultimately looks crass and clumsy when you come across as too pushy. You may as well just say 'Give me a job!'

Help! I don't know anybody

There is nothing more daunting than finding yourself in a room full of people you don't know. However, the purpose is solely to integrate yourself into the party and take home a fistful of business cards before the evening is out. In my network survival plan I like to stick to these rules: firstly, try to find out who is going and potentially if there is anybody you can initially approach (it could be a friend of a colleague), in which case it gives you someone to talk about and it breaks

the ice. Secondly, if you don't know a soul and find it hard breaking into a ring of people who are deep in conversation, then don't feel shy in asking the person who organised the event to introduce you. That's what they are there for.

Conversation starters

What's the best way of starting a conversation with a complete stranger? Remembering you are, to all intents and purposes, at work and not on a night out with the girls, your chit-chat needs to be fairly conservative. Boring as it may sound, play ultra-safe and initially chat about the surroundings, the food, the drinks, even the weather. Avoid anything confrontational, such as politics, religion and sex. Once you've built up a rapport with somebody you can then ask them, 'and what do you do?' giving you the opportunity to chat about work.

The art to successful networking is working the room. Once you've established a contact, make your excuses and leave. You don't have to look rude, simply touch them on the arm and say, 'Lovely to meet you, but I suppose I had better be moving on!' This way you sound genuine and, after all, if they are professional networkers themselves they will understand that the gathering is all about meeting lots of new people.

Keeping up

OK, you've got the contacts you needed, now what? I think there's no point keeping in touch with people if you don't like them. If you didn't bond with them, why would you want to work with or for them? Just keep in contact with people who (theoretically speaking) share your blood group! This way the outcome will more than likely be positive. The way in which you keep contact going is important: periodically drop emails asking how they are, what they've been up to, and so on. As you become friendlier you can then suggest meeting up for a coffee or a drink. This then leads to a more relaxed atmosphere, which makes networking all the more easier.

LIFE-LONG TIP

To help you keep track of everybody, make little notes on business cards you are given. It could be anything from 'bubbly brunette' to 'scary and loud' or 'creepy little man!'

A life lesson in loving being single

Sometimes it seems you can't escape the joy of coupledom. Everywhere you look – TV, ad campaigns, magazines – it's all about defining yourself as part of a happy-ever-after couple. Being in a relationship is often seen as wearing the badge of socially acceptable success, whereas being single is often unfairly seen as a negative state and something to be pitied. Rarely is it seen as a choice. Well, here's some news for those who think a grown-up girl can't be happy without a man.

Single and satisfied

Who's to say that flying solo should be the position you find yourself in only between boyfriends? Many of us make a choice to stay single purely to have a good time. Being single gives us an independence and freedom that a relationship cannot (however loved-up it might be). And, if coming out of a long-term or especially volatile relationship, it can be a life-saving and rejuvenating experience. In fact, it's said that one can't truly be successful in a relationship without living the single life for some time. Essentially you can use this state of independence to take full responsibility for yourself and become a more rounded person. It's surprising how much you end up compromising yourself and your values when coupled up.

Be your own boss (not bossed about)

This is the ideal time to do exactly what you want and be who you want. There is always compromise in a relationship – it's one of the rules for making it work, but while single you have no one to please and you don't have to answer to anybody. You can stay out, slob out on the sofa with unshaved legs and watch girlie DVDs for the twenty-fifth time. Who's stopping you? The great thing about being on your own is it gives you time to work out what you want from life, it's also a time to prove to yourself that you can lead a fulfilling and packed life without the help of any arm candy. Relationships usually add up to routine; being single equals spontaneity, so be daring while you can.

One of the nicest things about being on your own is being able to just take off when you feel like it. Why not book a week away at the last minute (it makes the whole experience more exciting), or do something out of the ordinary such as a parachute jump? In fact try anything where you don't have to double check with someone else. It can literally be the height of your freedom!

You can flirt for England

Being single frees you up to do different things and mix with different people. Invariably couples tend to stick to seeing other couples – and where's the flirt factor in that? (You don't want to upset another girl by winking saucily at her good-looking boyfriend do you?) When single you suddenly find yourself wearing a different overcoat: you feel liberated and more daring, so take that feeling and work it to the max! Flirt with anybody who takes your fancy (see the tips on page 96 if you find yourself a bit rusty) and remind yourself that you are perfectly free to encourage male attention. This makes you feel wanton and powerful, as being single allows you to have no-strings-attached (safe) sex with them if you so desire. Enjoy not having to explain your actions!

It's all about you

In the absence of a full-time relationship, you can focus on just one thing: yourself. (You can you revel in the fact that you don't have to tolerate his irritating habits such as picking his toenails in front of the television.) Relationships usually wind up a juggling act where you have to balance many things and pay equal attention to all of it. But in the lack of a significant other you can devote all your circus skills to yourself. You can give more time to your career, for example, and not worry about putting in those extra hours to impress your boss for moving-up-the-career-ladder gain. Make single life really work for you by redirecting all your energies into making yourself happy and successful in your own right.

LIFE-LONG TIP

★ Seek out restaurants with nice-looking waiters. Food and sex are the two most potent aphrodisiacs, and being single you can max the situation for all its worth!

A life lesson in handling a builder

Commissioning building work on your home is exciting – even if it isn't on a grand scale – because you're creating something that projects your own style. However, to get the best job done at the best price you need to turn into something of a project manager and remain actively involved throughout the whole process. Before anyone starts hammering, here's some solid advice.

Shopping for a builder

You've pored over glossy interior magazines, nosed into people's windows and searched the Internet for design ideas, and now you're ready to call in a bevy of gorgeous builders to turn your place into your very own palace. Shopping for a team of builders (or a builder) is not too dissimilar from shopping for a great haircut. If you have friends, relatives or neighbours who have had building work that you admire, ask them which builder they used and whether they would recommend him. After referrals invite at least three builders to provide quotes.

Take control from the start

You are the client and you need to act like it. Don't think the builder is doing you a favour by simply turning up; like staff in posh clothing boutiques, builders can have a horrible habit of intimidating you. Write up a detailed written specification of the work you want done – do not leave anything to chance. If you are having major works done, rather than, say, a set of shelves built, you will need to employ an architect to provide detailed drawings, which are required for planning and building approval. Make enough copies to give a full set to each of the builders you invite to quote for the works.

Emphasise to the builders that you want quotes to cover everything you would like to be done, including the materials and removal of any rubbish. When shopping for builders ask yourself (apart from their financial quote), 'Do I like them?' Remember: they will be in your personal space for weeks or

months so are they somebody you can stand to share your home with? Ask them questions, too – lots of them – and see how they respond. They should be knowledgeable about new building regulations (of which there are many) and building science issues. If they bat your questions away with comments like, 'Don't worry love, leave it to us,' perhaps you had better reconsider.

Lay down the rules

Bash out an agreed date to start and, more importantly, a finish date. If you are having a complete kitchen fitted, have a written list of the appliances to be installed complete with brands, model names and product numbers. You do not want the wrong pieces being delivered to your home. Do not pay any money up front before the work has begun. You can pay in instalments at the end of each phase if you are satisfied with the works.

Are they legal and bonded?

Before the walls start tumbling, make sure your contractor has obtained all of the approvals and paperwork required to begin building works. Make sure they are insured. Don't be shy in asking the building company for a copy of proof of their insurance.

LIFE-LONG TIP

★ *Don't leave your builders to 'just get on with it'. Don't go on holiday in the hope of coming back to a dream home. More than likely they will have been off-site for as many days as you were lying on the beach. Builders are like naughty children: they need to be kept an eye on at all times.*

CHAPTER 9
Work, Worries and (Ultimate) Well-being

A life lesson in managing your boss

Unless you decide to go for a new job, your boss is like a member of your family: you can't choose them! If you love your job, it pays to get along with your boss and make your personality rub along with theirs. The best you can do is to tap into their way of thinking and, therefore, put yourself on the road to work success.

Work out their personality

Believe it or not, your boss is human, however inhumane they can sometimes seem. And never forget: they hold your future in their hands! The first step is working out what makes them tick and getting inside their head. In short, you need to develop your emotional intelligence skills. Just like a box of chocolates, there are all different kinds of bosses, some with hard centres and some with soft, it's just a case of getting to grips with their ethics and work style. Remember: they are the boss and what they say (usually) goes, so learn how to communicate and 'read' them for team-building results. Track their moods. For example, are they: light hearted in the morning/grumpy in the afternoon/relaxed on Tuesday/ wound up on Thursday (board meeting)? Whatever they are, take note and angle your queries, ideas and suggestions accordingly and to your advantage.

Be a five-star employee (not a creep)

No boss likes an employee who gives him or her constant grief and questions their management style. Neither do they like someone who gratuitously butters them up by giving out false flattery in the hope of getting up the career ladder faster. The best employee is someone who works as a team player and who knows, or is willing to learn, the job inside out. Also, if faced with challenges (the management word for extra work above and beyond the call of your job description), put in the necessary work to get it done. However, if your boss is seemingly working 24 hours and he or she expects you to be on call day and night, you need to put them straight gently – after all they are paid to be a workaholic, you're not! Tell them you need time to relax and recharge your brain in order to work at your full potential. Don't be scared to air your views – in the best possible way!

Be popular but don't pal up with your boss

Work can be a fickle world and sometimes boundaries can become blurred, especially if it's an office culture that is very sociable. The general rule is not to become over-friendly with your superior – it can backfire in ways you hadn't expected. First off: as your confidence grows and you become recognised within the company your boss may get resentful and try to hold you back. After all, not only do you work for him or her, but you have become their confidante and if your boss depends on you too much (or you're privy to personal stuff about them that they would rather others didn't know about in the company) they won't put you forward for promotion. Obviously, if your boss asks you for lunch or a drink, don't turn them down, but keep it friendly and professional.

Keep in their good books

If you want to make headway in your company, then it pays not to wind your boss up. When it comes to gaining extra brownie points, it makes corporate sense to make their job easier. General rules are: don't be (consistently) late, don't take time off ill unless you are ill, don't hang out at the water cooler gossiping (especially about your boss) and make sure you're visible to them – even when you're not. Copy them in on important emails and let them know when you've completed work and are free to assist them on other projects. Ultimately, if your boss ends up with less stress due to you taking on more workload they'll see you as a superstar!

Don't take criticism personally

It's inevitable that at some time in your working life you are going to get criticised. It's only too easy to act like a wounded child and start to make excuses for your decisions or actions, but take it like a grown-up girl and don't alienate yourself. Acknowledge that negative feedback doesn't feel good and make a pact not to make it a regular thing. Think about what made your boss react the way he or she did and distance yourself from the situation. If you can view the criticism from a less personal point of view, you'll be able to look at it more constructively.

... and if you're a newly promoted boss

Being a boss isn't just about laying down the rules and shouting 'You're fired!' Donald Trump-style, it's about making staff feel valued. That way you reap better results. Remember: if you're a bad boss, then staff won't stick around and your superiors will begin to wonder why. To keep a happy workforce, criticise in private, but praise in public. Also, be up-front about company changes – employees will accept change more readily if consulted first – and command respect by showing good leadership skills while helping each member of your team personally to succeed as much as you can.

LIFE-LONG TIP

★ If you really can't get along with your boss, however hard you try, it may be best to leave. Your boss won't change his management style to suit you and may actually be holding you back. It's always best to leave before you come to personality blows, as there's nothing worse than relying on an ex-boss you've fallen out of favour with for your next reference.

A life lesson in getting promoted

Promotions don't automatically land on your desk according to how many years you've worked at the company, they have to be earned. Some career experts even say that you should start planning your promotion the minute you start a new position. Here's how to create opportunities and plot your going-up-the-ladder plan.

Boast about yourself – gracefully

Generally, women don't like bragging about themselves – after all, we're taught that modesty is a virtue, but if nobody knows how great you actually are what are the chances of getting ahead of those that bellow their fabulousness from the rooftops? And if you thought all your hard work surely wouldn't go unnoticed by the powers that be, then think again. Chances are your boss(es) are way too busy juggling 101 things at once to notice the girl who always has her head down when they sweep around the office president-style. Two words: sell yourself. You don't even have to be an all-out show-girl about it. Say something to your boss such as, 'I'm thrilled that the presentation we made won us our newest and most sought-after client, it was really worth my while putting in all those extra hours,' then you won't come across as a hard-nosed bragger. Let it be known you're up for promotion. After all, you can't expect your boss to be Mystic Meg – sometimes you just have spell it out.

Find yourself a mentor

It's been revealed that four out of five promotions are given to those who seek out a mentor. Establishing a bond with some-body who's a rung or two further up the career ladder than you can be really helpful when it comes to advising you on how to get ahead. I've had many mentors in my working life whom I owe great thanks to for giving me their advice when I wanted it – and when I didn't want to hear it. Your mentor could be anyone: a successful friend who wants you to succeed, your dad's boss, a previous boss or even an old university lecturer. Find one you can trust and they can really be a guiding spirit.

Go the extra mile

Doing your job well will undoubtedly impress. But go the extra mile and your superiors will begin to sit up and take notice. Look at your job in the same way an actor would a performance: if you want a standing ovation you need to put your heart and soul into it. Be go-getterish, too. Sound ener-gised and excited when your boss asks you how things are going, and put yourself forward for acquiring new skills.

Never forget that knowledge is power, so it goes without saying that one of the best ways to get yourself on top of the promotion list is to expand your job skills, whether it's getting to know the new technology or learning team-leading skills. Seek out evening classes if you have to. Ultimately, the more skills you notch up the more marketable you will become. Even if promotion doesn't come this time, the chances are you'll be in line for a pay rise!

Get yourself a reputation

… for being the best. Stay sharp in your job and it will pay off. If you're serious about the P word, then dress professionally – or suited to your job. If you're working in a solicitor's office, for example, don't take dress-down Friday too literally. Leave the midriff-baring top for the weekend. If working in advertising, wear jeans but don't make your look too down-and-out. Don't get drawn into office tittle-tattle, as it can rock your reputation with your boss, and far from being a whiner when things go pear-shaped, turn yourself into a problem solver.

Daring to be different and working on your own initiative always goes down well (as long as you're confident in what you're doing). If a nail-nibbling situation crops up, be sure to come up with at least a couple of problem solvers before hunting out your boss's what-should-we-do-next scenario. And finally, it may sound Scout-like but … be prepared and stay alert: nothing says 'not interested' quite so clearly as falling asleep on the job.

A life lesson in being freelance

Going freelance is a big step, as although it means getting rid of office politics (hurrah!) it also means setting yourself up as self-employed, which can be a nail-biting thought in itself. The world of freelance can be unpredictable and insecure, but above all it can be exciting, so here's how to make not going out to work steady work for you.

A true life story

I used to have a 'proper' job: I worked on magazines, where I breezily banked a healthy pay cheque every month, had fun work colleagues and received many perks. Now, I'm a freelance writer as well as moonlighting as a bookkeeper/tea girl/secretary and general dogsbody. I don't have private health insurance or a company-run pension plan, and not everybody promptly returns my calls or emails, and my bank account has certainly sometimes seen better days. It may sound crazy, but I'm happy. I wasn't shoved into the ranks of freelancers through being made redundant or getting the elbow, I decided to give up my much sought-after position to scare myself into seeking out different kinds of writing work. It has paid off. But before I get too smug, let me tell you that it's not always an easy ride and not everybody is suited to the freelance life.

When first starting out it can be like rubbing two sticks together to start a fire: it takes patience and time to see a glimmer of hope. You need to see and sell yourself as a 'brand', be flexible and prepared to smile when you want to grimace. 'Yes, no problem,' becomes your catchphrase to seemingly far-stretched demands, and above all you need to have a strong sense of self. Knockbacks can be fast and furious so there's an increased responsibility to succeed, and it can be lonely at times, particularly if you're home based.

You get rid of your boss – and gain three more!

The common belief with freelance is that you wave goodbye to your boss and you're the one in charge. Not so. This is a free-lance fallacy; the truth of the matter is you gain as many bosses as you have clients. OK, so you don't have to see them every day and they're not giving you the evil eye every five minutes when your report is late, but be prepared for having to tune into a huge range of personalities, management styles and corporate cultures if you want the taste of regular success.

Don't just rely on talent

It's a common belief that your skills and talent will effortlessly lead to piles of good work. Again, not true. Of course, talent in your field counts, but being freelance is also a social skill. When seeking commissions, you need to bring in the 'schmooze' factor – sound enthusiastic about the project (however boring it sounds) and make them feel they're your only client – even if you've got other deadlines going on. Think about it. If a client has a choice of hiring someone who seems reluctant and picks up on all the negative aspects of the job, or somebody who seems genuinely pleased and enthusiastic to get the job, who they gonna cherry-pick?

Build up a freelance buddy system

One of the big losses when you go out alone is losing the day-to-day contact with your work friends. It can be isolating working from home or going into offices where you know not a soul. To save your sanity it's essential to build up a freelance network – people that are in the same boat as you. I have valuable freelance friends, all of whom are on my speed dial and who I wouldn't be without. I call them my virtual office as we give one another a call if we're feeling rejected (often), elated (sometimes) or when we just want to bounce ideas off each other.

Make your workspace workable

One of the big mistakes would-be freelancers make is not taking their 'office' seriously. Far from setting up your empire on your bed, you need a proper desk and enough space to make you perform functionally and professionally. Make it personal and cheery – like you couldn't in an office. Use colourful pens for boring paperwork and make an inspiration board and fill it with pictures. To make myself work harder, I always put up pictures of my last holiday and think to myself, 'Work hard and you can bliss out in Bali next year or have fun in Florida!'

> ### LIFE-LONG TIP
> ★ *Freelance is famously known for being feast-or-famine, so before you chuck in your notice, put out feelers and start making connections. Save at least six months' earnings from the salary you are currently getting. Companies are not always prompt at paying, and if you don't have a financial net then things can get tricky.*

A life lesson in giving yourself a voice

Don't underestimate the power (that's pitch and tone) of your voice when it comes to getting what you want at work. The pace and personality of your voice literally speaks volumes about who you are. Whether you're giving a presentation, a speech or on an important call, it pays to watch your mouth.

Your voice: what it says about you

We all know somebody who is boring to listen to, but ask yourself: is it what they're saying or the tone of their voice? It's all very well if you're dressed to impress, but how do you sound? In the work world, and in social circles, the impression you make is largely by how you sound. Studies show that your voice leaves a more lasting impression than your appearance. Unfair as it seems, we make judgements in life purely based on appearance and the sound of somebody's voice. And that can affect how you're seen (or heard) at work and in life generally. Even the most beautiful people can be let down by their voice.

Lower your tone

If pitched just right a voice can be seductive, not only in the bedroom but in the workplace, too. Most of us don't want to sound like we're straight out of theatre school, but wouldn't it be great to sound more interesting (even if what you're saying isn't) and more compelling just by altering the pitch of our voice? According to voice coaches, one of the most common vocal faults is to project at a higher pitch than naturally fits the voice. This can make you sound like Betty Boop. I decided to tweak my vocal cords consciously after someone told me I sounded nine when answering the phone – definitely not the image I want to project!

There's no great science in lowering your voice, you simply need to heighten your awareness of diaphragmatic breathing. A voice that sounds thin, high and tinny is usually starved of air. But begin to breathe deeply, so that your lungs fill out, and your voice will take on a deeper resonance. And don't feel you have to rush everything out in one speedy sentence. Take your time in saying what you want – a well-paced speaker will sound confident and calm, which makes people listen. Those that sound like a speed freak lose their authority, as their sentences start losing impact. They start to use lots of 'ums' and 'ahs' as their need is increased to gulp in air.

Have a good phone voice

As phone calls have frequently taken the place of meet and greets in the workplace, our voices have taken on more significance. We've all struck up a rapport with people on the telephone that we've never met and have conjured up in our heads what we think they look like based purely on their voice. So ask yourself: what does your voice say about you? I think, more than anything, that your voice needs to sound friendly, energetic and direct. What's the point pitching for a job if you sound flat and uninterested? Before an important call, smile – it will make the tone of your voice sound warmer – and exercise your mouth by mouthing the vowels and wiggling your tongue about. Lazy lips and a tense tongue can result in a badly produced voice that sounds mumbled and gargled. Finally, drink lots of water and avoid coffee – it saps moisture from your vocal cords.

Watch your posture

The best voices come from those with good alignment. Straighten up and you automatically loosen up the neck and throat areas. Ultimately, a saggy body will equal a saggy and weak-sounding voice! It is particularly important to position the head over the shoulders rather than commonly jutting it forwards or tilting it backwards. Don't think you have to sit at a desk to have a conversation either. Standing up and waving your arms about as you would if talking face-to-face will make you sound energised and confident not only in your voice but in your manner, too.

LIFE-LONG TIP

★ *Everybody hates listening to the sound of their own voice, but if you want to improve on it, read a passage of a book into a tape recorder, play it back and decide what needs working on: pitch, pace or personality.*

A life lesson in increasing your fertility

Whether you're ready to baby shop tomorrow or next year, it makes sense to know how to maximise your fertility today. One in six couples are reported to have problems conceiving, so, if you're lucky, getting pregnant means chucking out your contraception, indulging in lots of sex where a sperm quickly meets an egg and makes a baby. For others it can take months or even years for their body to make a baby.

Get checked for chlamydia

It's not nice talking about sexually transmitted infections (STIs) but they have to be faced when talking fertility. One in ten women is said to be infected with chlamydia, which is a very common STI caused by a bacteria-like organism in the urethra and reproductive system. The thing is, chlamydia is sneaky because when it comes to talking symptoms there aren't any. But if left undetected infection can damage the fallopian tubes, which are the transport system for your eggs from the ovaries to the womb. If left undiagnosed, chlamydia can lead to pelvic inflammatory disease (PID), which can scar the reproductive organs.

So are you at risk? The more sexually active you are or have been with different partners, the more you are at risk, so put your mind at rest and do a two-minute test. You are not routinely tested for chlamydia while having a smear test, so you have to request it separately. Tests have now been developed that are done on urine samples, which makes testing for it less cringeworthy than having a smear. If detected in the early stages it is easily treatable with antibiotics.

Is your cycle monthly?

If your periods are all over the place try to find out why. One possible explanation could be polycystic ovary syndrome (PCOS), which upsets and shakes about hormones, stopping the ovaries from releasing eggs. If this is diagnosed you may need hormone medication to become pregnant. And don't leave very painful periods unchecked either. This could be endometriosis, which is where the uterine lining grows outside the womb, and can potentially damage the reproductive organs. Again, medication can help, and in extreme cases laser surgery can help to reverse the problem.

Be aware of your body fat

There is a strong relationship between body fat and fertility. Being too thin or too heavy can hinder your chances of getting pregnant – for both sexes. But it's not just a matter of the number on the scales. Doctors are finding it's not necessarily your weight that could be stopping you from conceiving, but your body fat. A woman must have body fat of at least 18 per cent to produce oestrogen leading to ovulation. Your best chance of making a baby is when 20–25 per cent of your body mass is fat tissue. Getting this balance right makes for the baby bingo factor, as thin women may have too little oestrogen and overweight women too much to become pregnant.

Keep an eye on your man, too. Thin men, such as those who run hard and fast, may have low sperm counts, whereas over-weight men can have low testosterone levels and high oestrogen levels, which impede the production of sperm. To calculate your body mass index (BMI) divide your weight in kilograms by your height in metres squared. In the meantime, it goes without saying that you should both keep your diets as balanced and as fresh as possible.

The little incidentals

Fertility can be a complicated old business, especially for something that is supposed to be natural, but 21st-century living is to blame. Too much coffee, for example, is said to have a negative effect on fertility, so cut down on caffeine at least three months before getting baby jiggy with it. Research into the fertility of men who regularly carry and use mobile phones has also raised concerns. It's been suggested that their sperm count might be cut by up to 30 per cent, so encourage him to use a landline!

Stress is also an excellent contraceptive. Both the male and female hormonal systems are affected by stress. Stress in women disrupts the hormonal conversation between the brain, the pituitary gland and the ovaries, interfering with both the maturation of an egg and the ovulation process. In the case of men, both physical and emotional stresses are known to rock his fertility. The answer? Try to chill out together, whether it's giving each other a pampering massage or curling up in front of the television.

LIFE-LONG TIP

★ If all else fails take a holiday! Apparently a baby can be your ultimate souvenir when holidaying in warmer climes. Not only do holidays melt stress away with the ice cream, but also sunlight is one of the best fertility treatments around. Numerous studies indicate that fertility and sex drives increase when sunlight is intense as well as encouraging regular ovulation in women.

A life lesson in boosting your immune system

Your immune system is your body's military armour, as it's your first line of defence against potentially harmful invaders – from a cold to a bee sting to more serious issues such as cancer. Here are ways you can put up a healthy fight.

Listen to music you love

Music that really rocks your world can give your immune system one big lift. Scientists have revealed that tuning into tunes that send 'shivers down your spine' activates the same feel-good parts of the brain that are activated by food and sex. In fact, why not double your immunity insurance by listening to your favourite tracks while having sex? One study carried out by psychologists in Pennsylvania revealed that people who get jiggy with music once or twice a week showed higher levels of immunoglobulin A – an antigen found in saliva that some scientists use to evaluate how strong our immune systems are.

Be a party girl

The more sociable you are, the stronger your immune system will be. Studies have revealed that people with the most diverse social contacts were least affected when exposed to the common cold. If you don't want to be in bed with a bottle of cold remedy, accept every invitation going! It's even been suggested that lack of socialising poses as much of a threat to your immunity as being overweight and smoking. Put in some huggy power, too. Giving or receiving big bear hugs can boost the activity of the natural killer cells that seek out and obliterate cancer cells or cells that have been invaded by nasty viruses. Consider marriage proposals, too. Studies show that married people have stronger immune systems than singletons. But then again, that's only if you're happily married – so consider carefully!

Exercise, but not too hard

Although regular workouts are generally deemed a good thing – even if they don't feel like it – moderation is the key. Over-exercising like a demented gym bunny can actually inhibit the efficient functioning of your immune system by weakening your body's responses to disease. One study found that marathon runners who ran more than 60 miles a week had twice as many upper respiratory infections as those who ran fewer than 20 miles a week. Even if you can't see yourself running a couple of miles, it does make sense to relate these findings to any type of exercise done to extreme whether it be cycling, swimming or aerobics.

Customise your supplements

The latest way to winterise your health and ward off the dreaded cold and flu season is by customising your supplements. It's a process known as synergy, and once you know which supplements work well together you can create your very own superbooster. A combination that strengthens your immune system is the Chinese herb astragalus, which becomes even more powerful when you take it with echinacea. Another combination to mix 'n' match is vitamin C and zinc. As commonly known, vitamin C builds up the body's resistance to colds, but it performs more efficiently if you take it with zinc – a mineral that acts synergistically with the vitamin to protect and strengthen blood vessels. For best advice, seek help from a pharmacist or herbalist.

Have a curry!

A hot curry is packed full of ingredients that can help treat the symptoms of a cold by strengthening the body's immune system. Capsaicin – the compound that makes chillies hot – encourages your body to make more antibodies, thus bolstering up the immune system. Create a defensive diet, too. Orange vegetables such as sweet potatoes, orange peppers, carrots and pumpkins are a rich source of vitamin A, which helps to protect the skin from free radicals. The skin is often neglected, but crucially it's the body's first line of defence against infection. Infections reach the body through the lungs via the skin.

LIFE-LONG TIP

★ Have a DNA day. That's busy Doing Nothing at All! Get stressed and your immune system starts to falter and collapse. Stress sends your body's production of cortisol and adrenaline into overdrive – hormones that lower your immune response.

Never stop growing up

Is your life sorted now? Of course not, because I don't profess to know all the answers to life (who does?). And, although I'm sure these chapters have been invaluable to you they won't have addressed all of your wants/worries/wishes. Now you've finished reading this book from cover-to-cover (and I think it's a book that should always be kept within easy reach as these life 'n' style chapters are designed to be dipped in and out of frequently) you should continue to be open to take on board any extra nuggets of well meaning advice and suggestions that happen to come your way. The more you're open to new ideas and different ways of thinking the fuller and richer your life will quickly become.

Index